# Peterborough Ontario Book 2 in Colour Photos, Saving Our History One Photo at a Time

## Photography
by Barbara Raué
2015

## Series Name:
Cruising Ontario

## Book 100: Peterborough Book 2

Cover photo:  George Street Clock Tower downtown

# Series Name: Cruising Ontario
# Saving Our History One Photo at a Time
# in colour photos

# Other Books by Barbara Raue

Coins of Gold

Arrows, Indians and Love

The Life and Times of Barbara
Volume 1: Inventions That Have Enhanced My Life
Volume 2: Entertainment That I Have Enjoyed
Volume 3: East Coast Trips
Volume 4: Olympics Have Always Intrigued Me
Volume 5: Wonders of the World
Volume 6: Caribbean Cruises We Have Enjoyed
Volume 7: Animals
Volume 8: Storms and Other Major Disasters in My Lifetime
Volume 9: Wars, Terrorist Attacks and Major Disasters

The Cromwell Family Book

Laura Secord Discovered

Daddy Where Are You?

Visit Barbara's website to view all of her books
http://barbararaue.ca

# Peterborough

Peterborough is a city on the Otonabee River in central Ontario, 125 kilometres (78 miles) northeast of Toronto. Peterborough's nickname of "The Electric City" underscores the historical and present day importance of technology and manufacturing as an economic base of the city which has operations from large multi-national companies such as Seimans, Rolls Royce, and General Electric. Peterborough is known as the gateway to the Kawarthas, "cottage country", a large recreational region of the province. In 1818, Adam Scott settled on the west shore of the Otonabee River and the following year he began construction of a sawmill and gristmill, establishing the area as Scott's Plains. The mill was located at the foot of present-day King Street and was powered by water from Jackson Creek.

The year 1825 marked the arrival of 1,878 Irish immigrants from the city of Cork, a British Parliament experimental emigration plan to transport poor Irish families to Upper Canada. The scheme was managed by Peter Robinson, a politician in York (present-day Toronto). Scott's Plains was renamed Peterborough in his honour. The Irish emigrated from the Emerald Isle to escape over-crowding, poverty, political unrest, religious tensions, disease and the potato famine. By 1851 almost half of the town of Peterborough claimed Irish ancestry. They cleared the land in the rolling hills of the Peterborough countryside.

In 1845, Sandford Fleming, inventor of Standard Time and designer of Canada's first postage stamp, moved to the city to live with Dr. John Hutchison and his family, staying until 1847. Dr. John Hutchison was one of Peterborough's first resident doctors.

Beginning in the late 1850s, a canoe building industry grew up in and around Peterborough. The Peterborough Canoe Company was founded in 1893, with the factory being built on the site of the original Adam Scott mill. From 1928–36 the Johnson Motor Company/Outboard Marine (the makers of motorized boat engines) was established as an outgrowth of the original industry.

Peterborough was one of the first places in the country to begin generating hydro electrical power (even before the plants at Niagara Falls). Companies like Edison General Electric Company (later Canadian General Electric) and America Cereal Company (later to become Quaker Oats, and in 2001 PepsiCo, Inc.), opened to take advantage of cheap hydro-electric power.

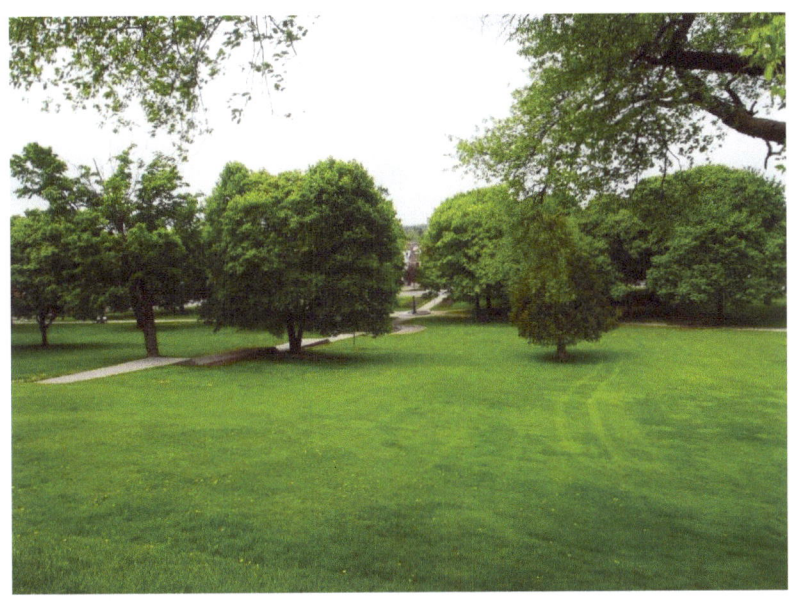

Water Street - Victoria Park

# Table of Contents

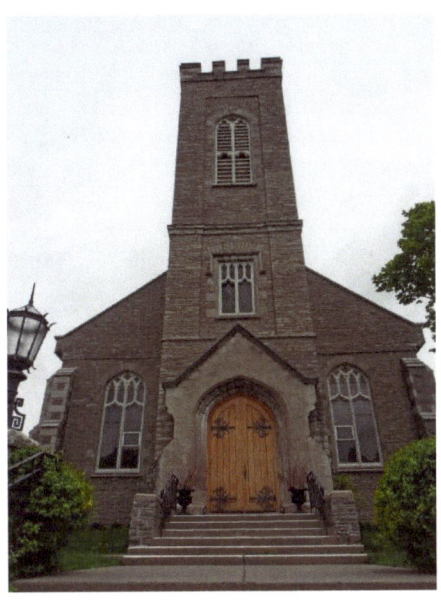

99 Brock Street - St. John's Anglican Church – established in 1826 - Peterborough's oldest church, completed in 1837, in Early English Gothic Revival architecture, in continuous use since its opening

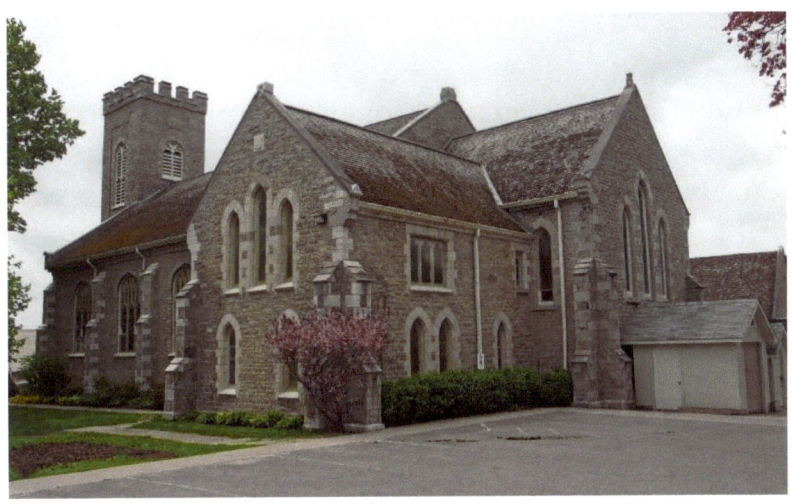

Buttresses, lancet windows

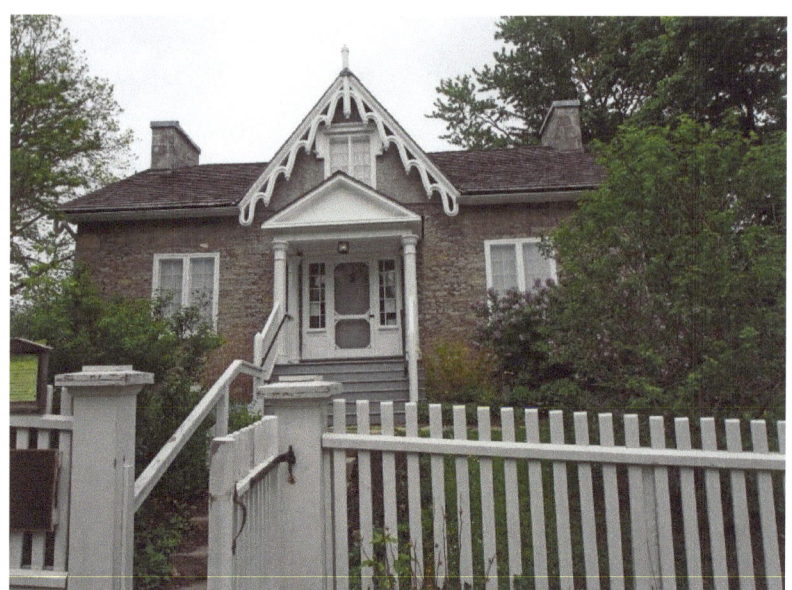

270 Brock Street - Hutchison House is one of the oldest limestone houses in Peterborough. It is in the Gothic Revival style with verge board trim and finial on the gable. It was built in 1837 for Dr. John Hutchison, the city's first resident physician. One of the bedrooms is dedicated to, Sir Sandford Fleming, a cousin of Dr. Hutchison, who lived in the house when he came to Canada in 1845, at 18 years old. The Hutchisons lived in the house until 1847, when Dr. Hutchison died of typhus he contracted from his patients. In 1851, the house was sold to James Harvey, a prominent local merchant and remained in the Harvey family until 1969, when it was donated to the Peterborough Historical Society. The house was restored to the mid -1800s period and opened as Hutchison House Living Museum in 1978.

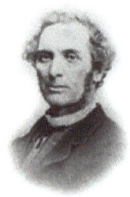

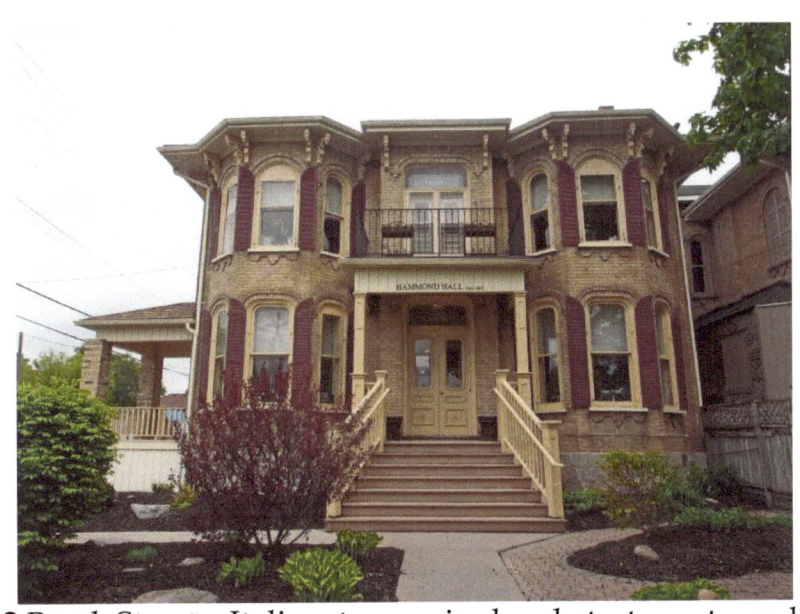

232 Brock Street – Italianate, cornice brackets, two-storey bay windows, second floor balcony

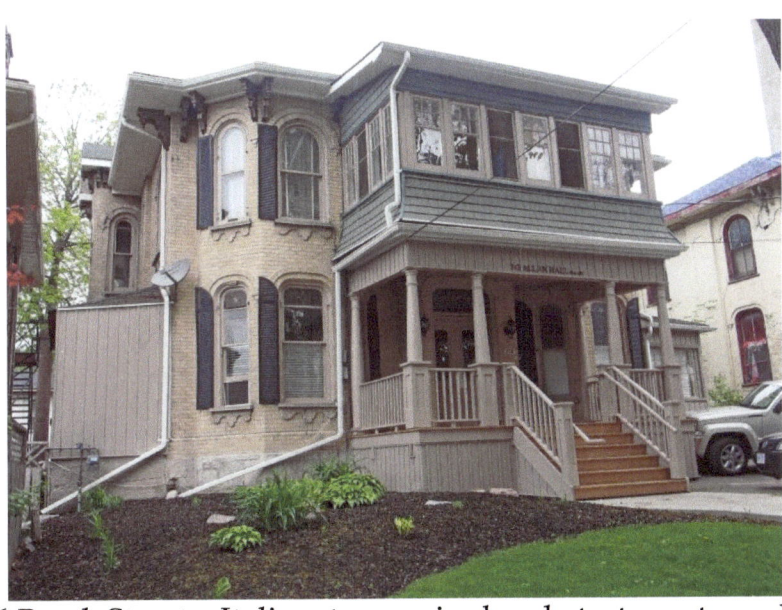

226 Brock Street – Italianate, cornice brackets, two-storey bay windows, second floor balcony

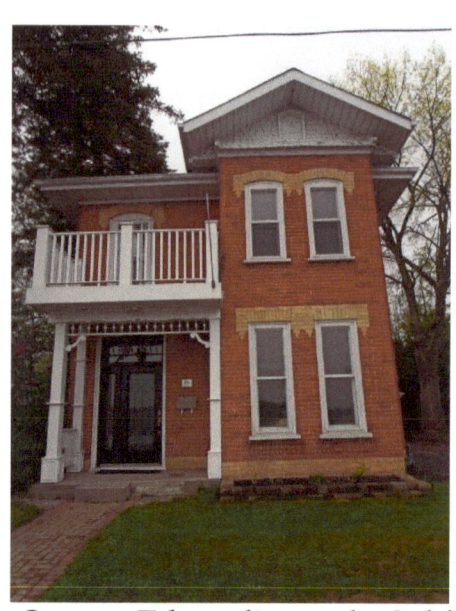

#45 Crescent Street – Edwardian style, 2nd floor balcony

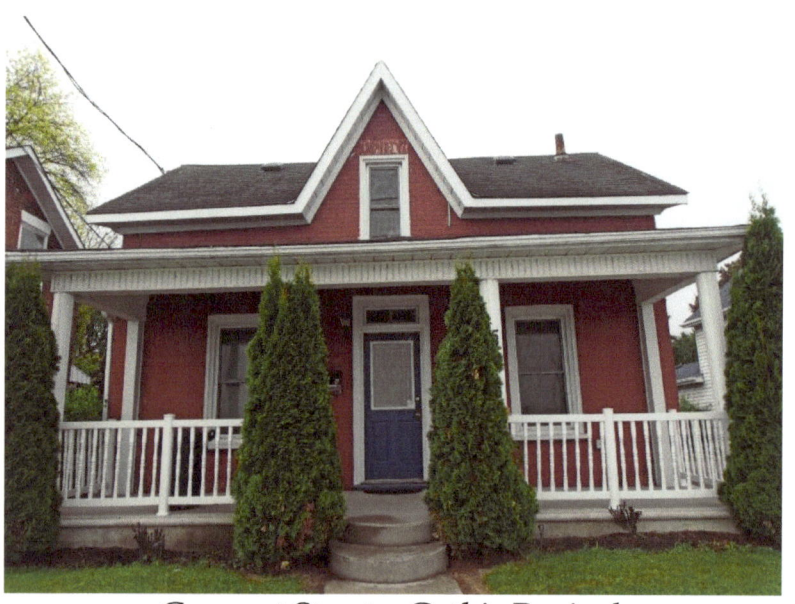

Crescent Street – Gothic Revival

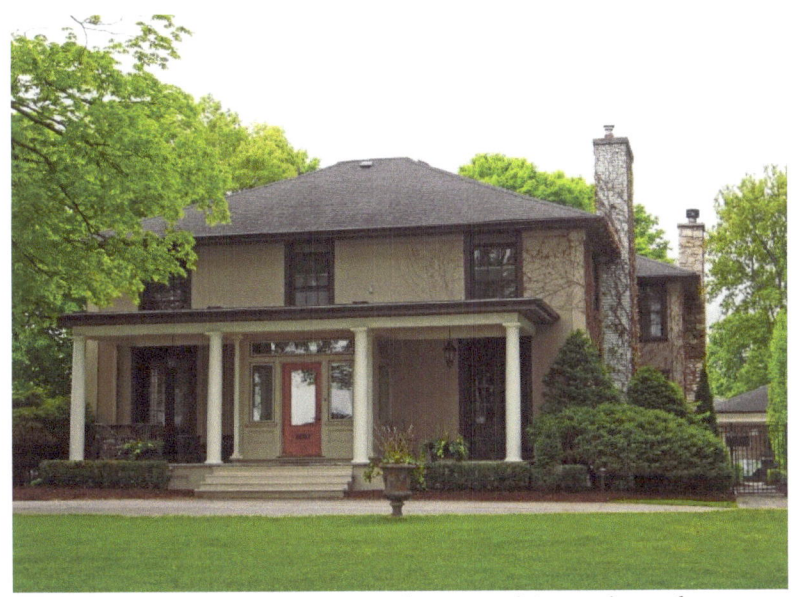

Crescent Street – Italianate, hipped roof

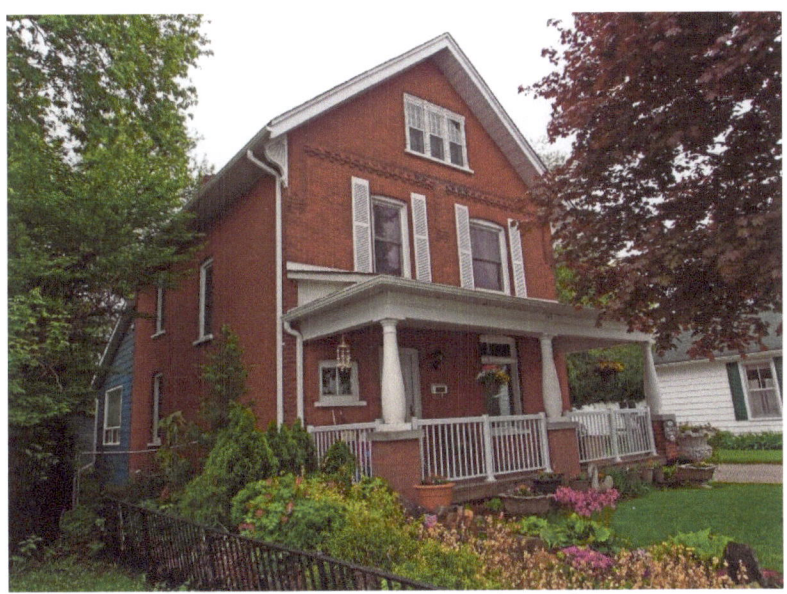

147 Crescent Street - Edwardian

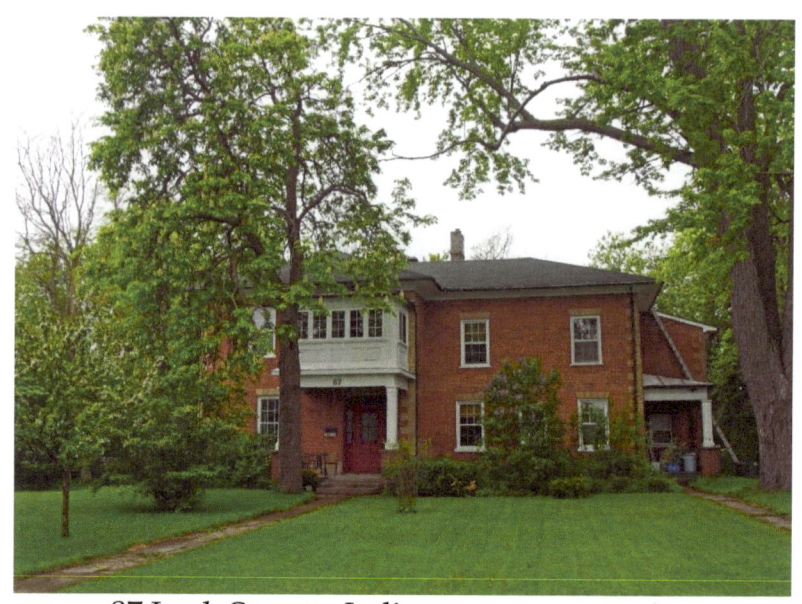

87 Lock Street – Italianate, corner quoins

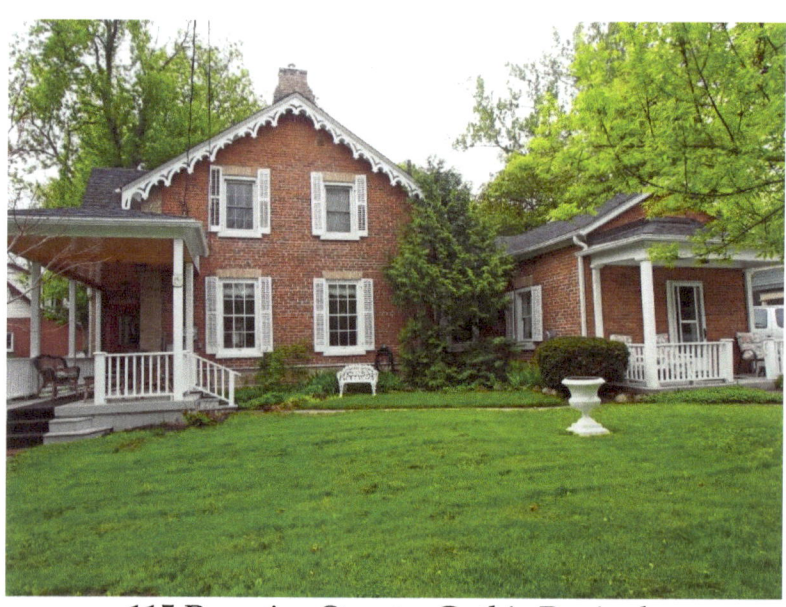

115 Romaine Street – Gothic Revival,
verge board trim on gable

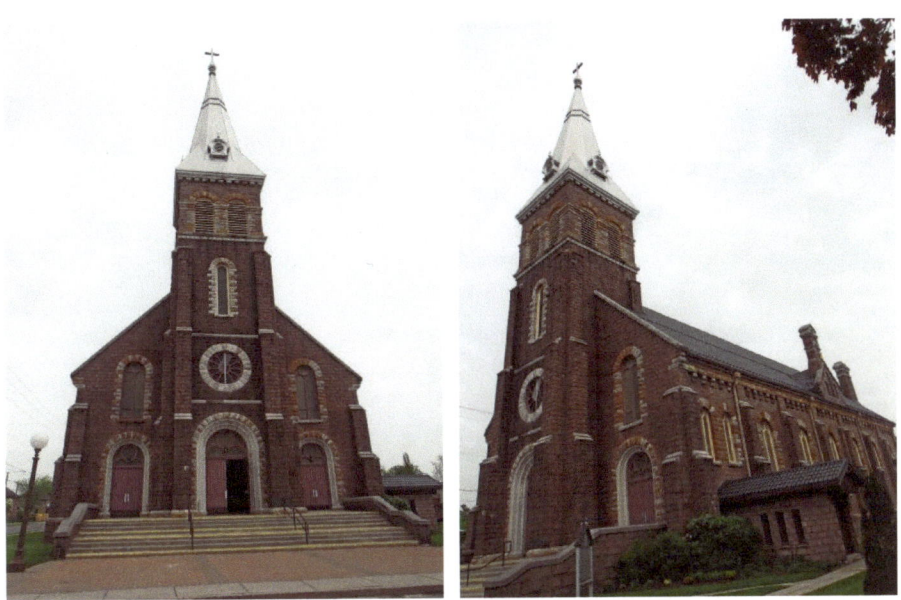

208 Romaine Street - Sacred Heart of Jesus founded 1909
Romanesque style

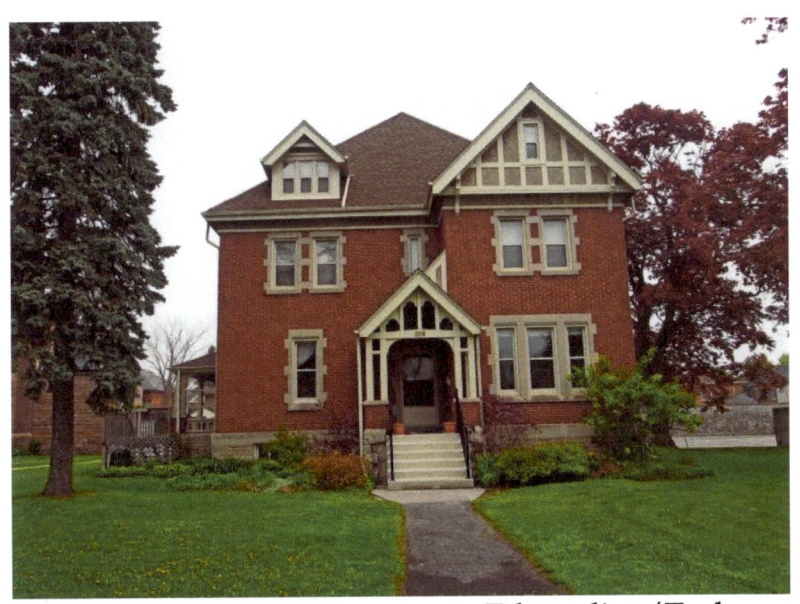

#208 Romaine Street – manse, Edwardian/Tudor

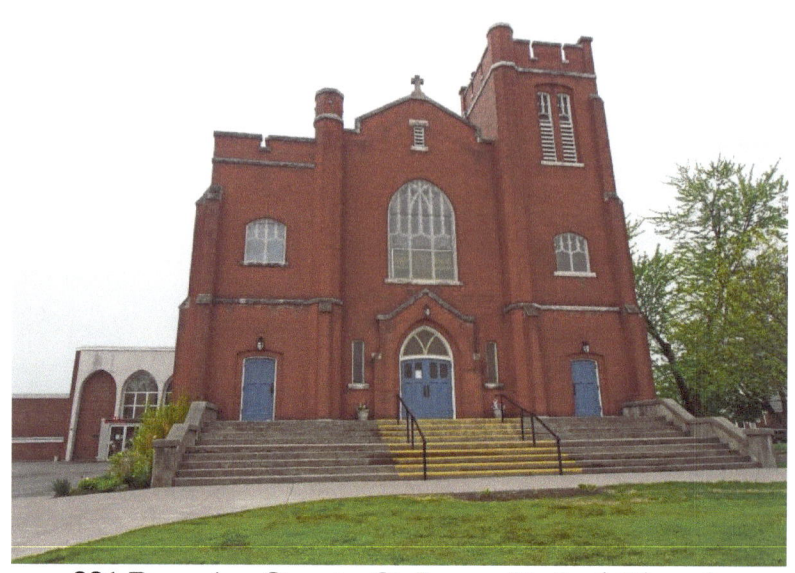

221 Romaine Street - St. James United Church

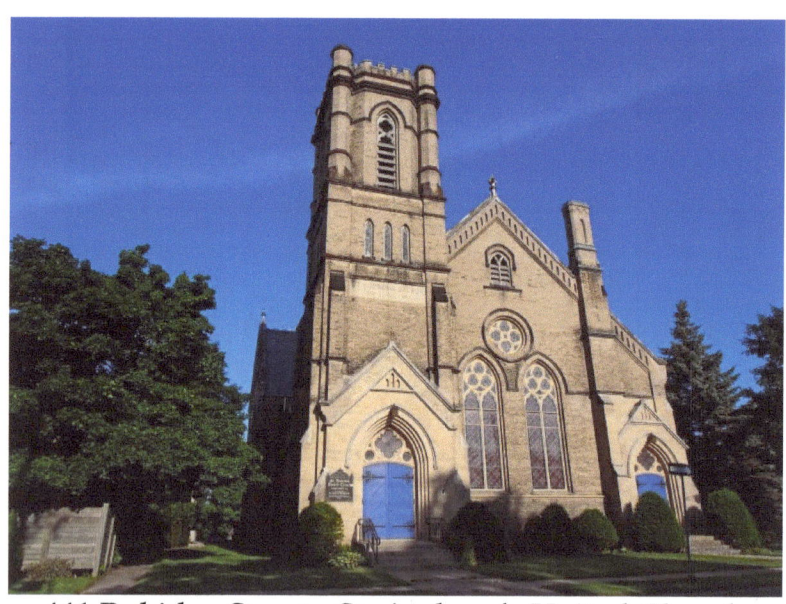

441 Rubidge Street - St. Andrew's United Church

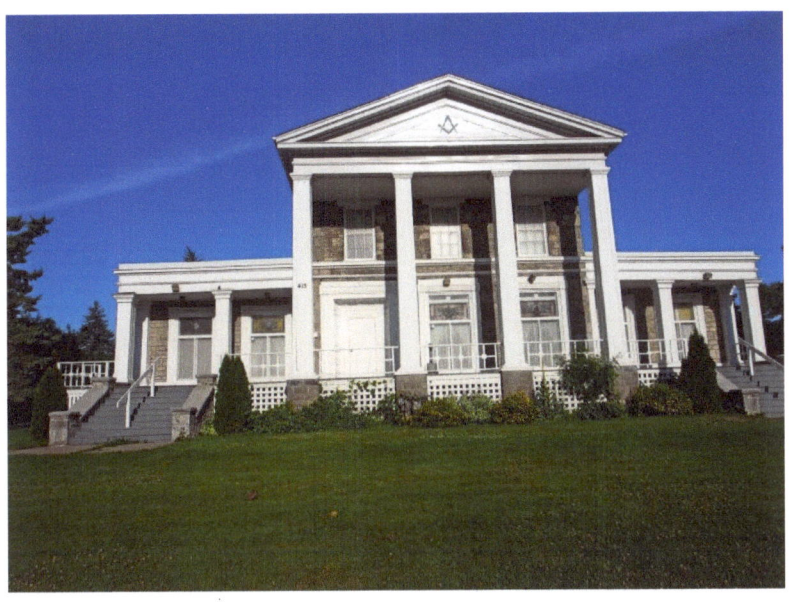

413 Rubidge Street - Grover Nichols House – an outstanding example of Greek Revival architecture, modified in the Palladian manner, it was begun about 1847 by P.M. Grover, a well-to-do local merchant.  The square pillars are a Classical Greek feature.  The local Masonic Lodge held its meetings here from 1849 to 1853 and the Masons purchased this imposing house in 1950.

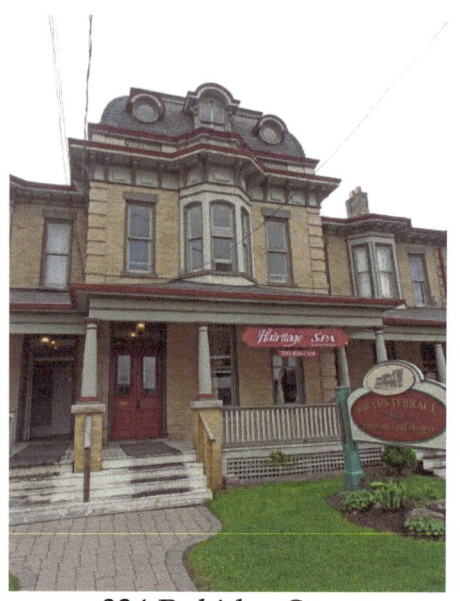 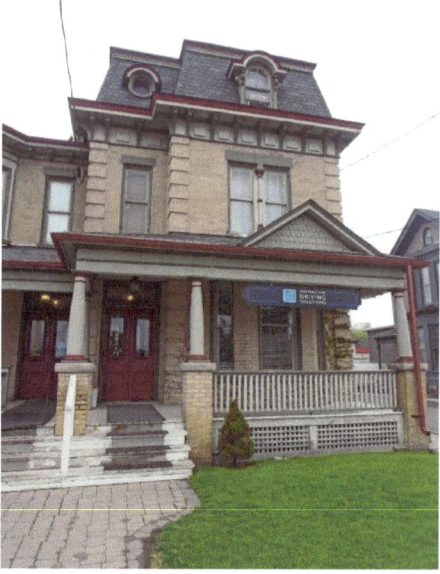

334 Rubidge Street     332  Rubidge Street

An elegant example of a residential terrace in the Second
Empire style, Cox Terrace, 332-344 Rubidge Street, was
constructed in 1884 during a time of prosperity and rapid
urban growth in Peterborough.  In this row of houses,
inspired by British models, seven dwellings are skillfully
unified behind one façade with three projecting pavilions.
Mansard roofs, dormers, and oriel windows give life to the
distinctive design.  The terrace was built for Sir George Cox,
one of the wealthiest and most influential Canadian
businessmen of the period.

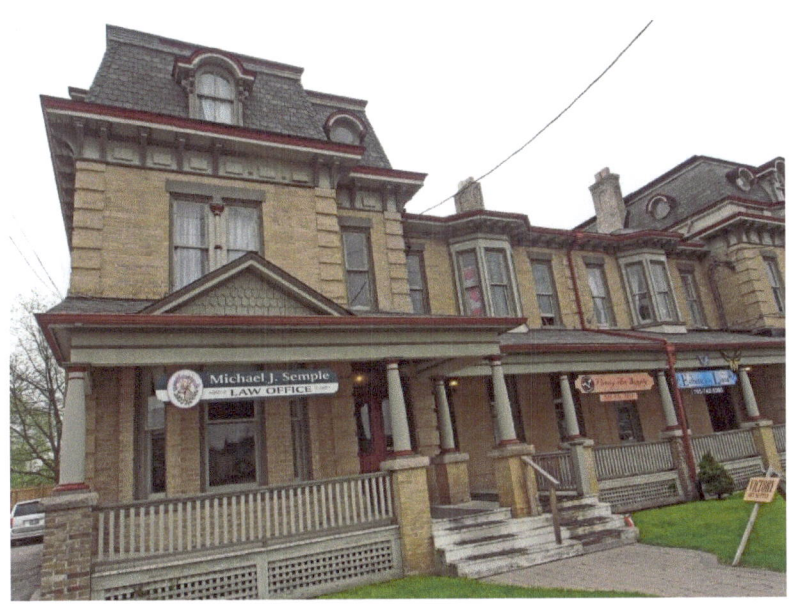

338 Rubidge Street

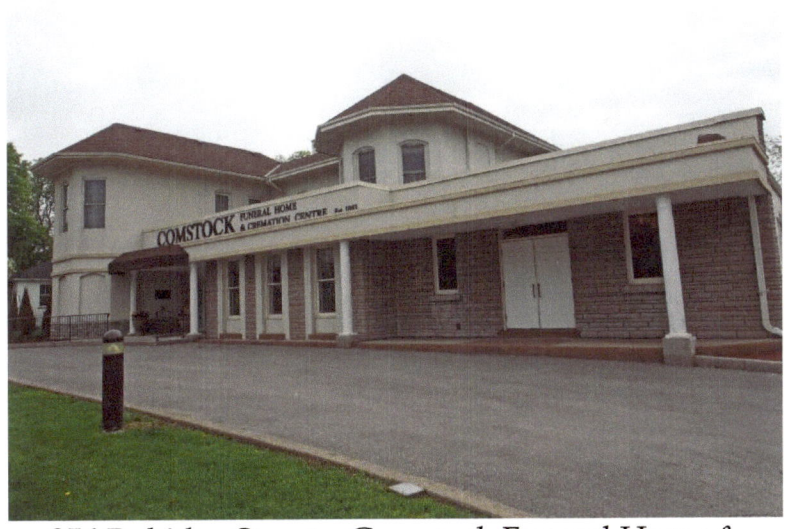

356 Rubidge Street – Comstock Funeral Home &
Cremation Centre – established 1853

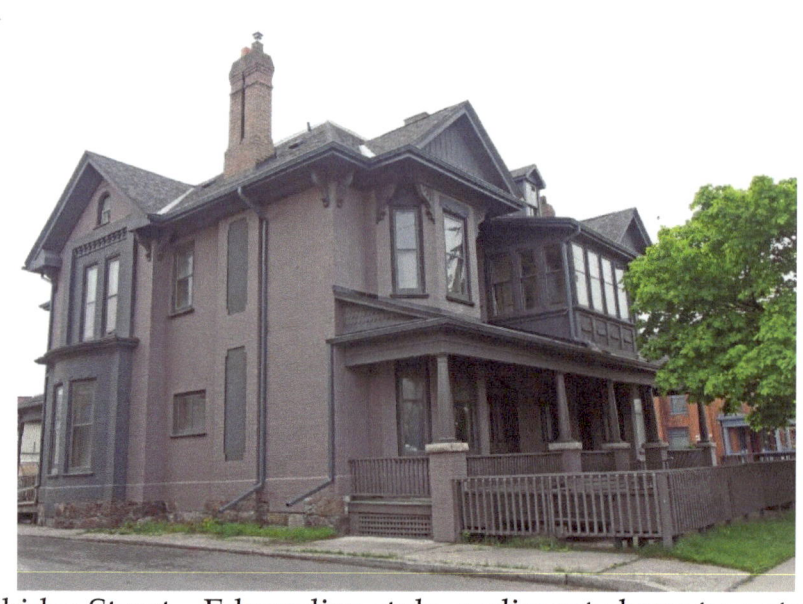

Rubidge Street – Edwardian style, pediment above two-storey bay window, second floor sunroom with dormer above

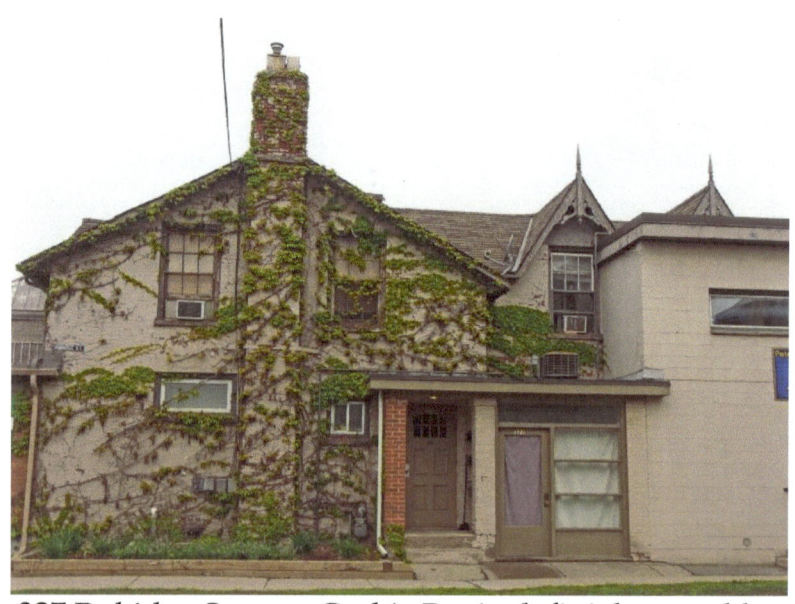

327 Rubidge Street – Gothic Revival, finials on gables

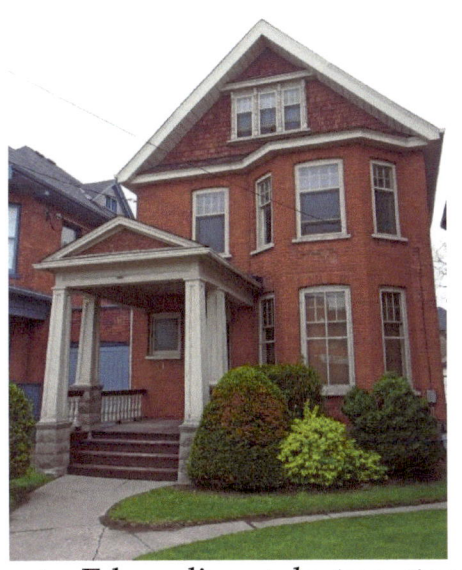

312 Rubidge Street – Edwardian style, two-storey bay window

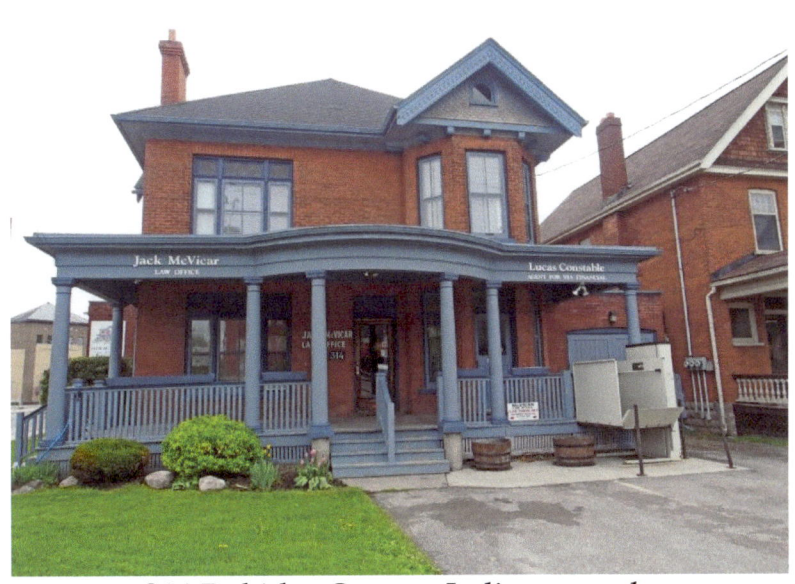

314 Rubidge Street – Italianate style
with 2½ storey tower-like bay

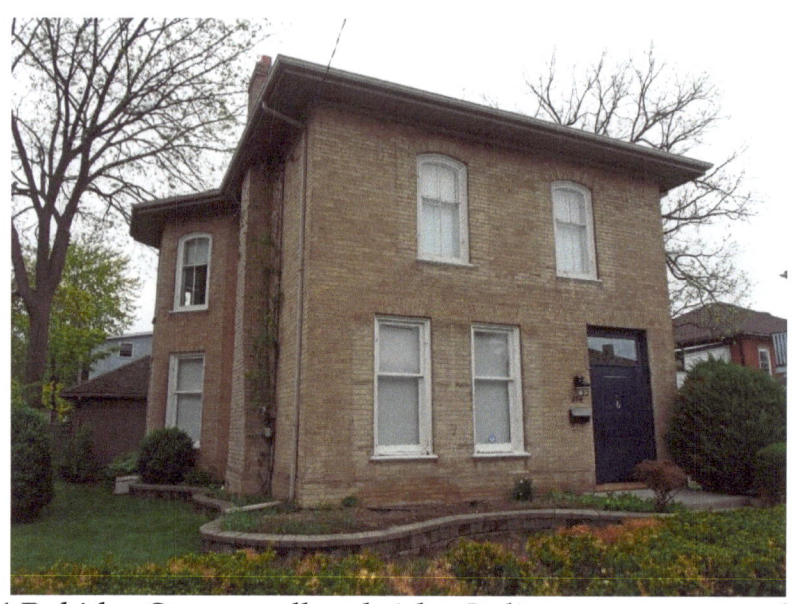

294 Rubidge Street - yellow brick – Italianate, two-storey bay window on side

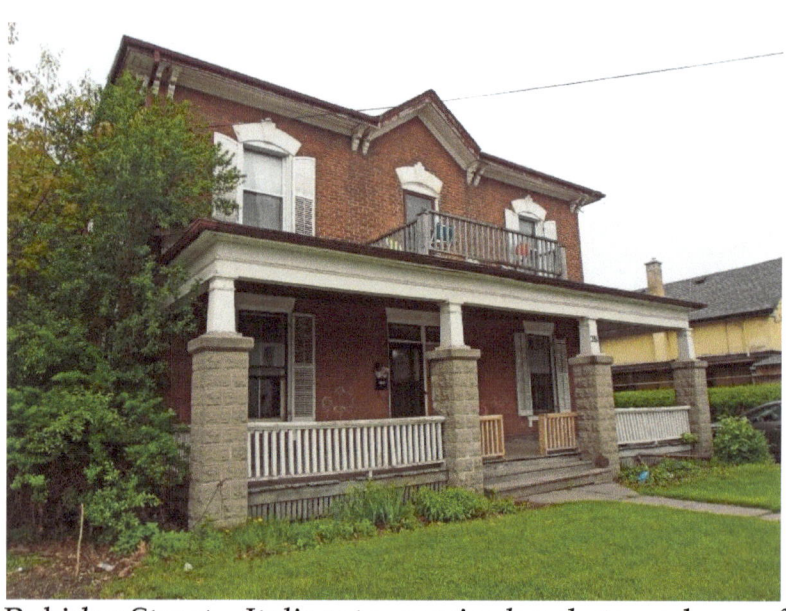

281 Rubidge Street – Italianate, cornice brackets under roofline

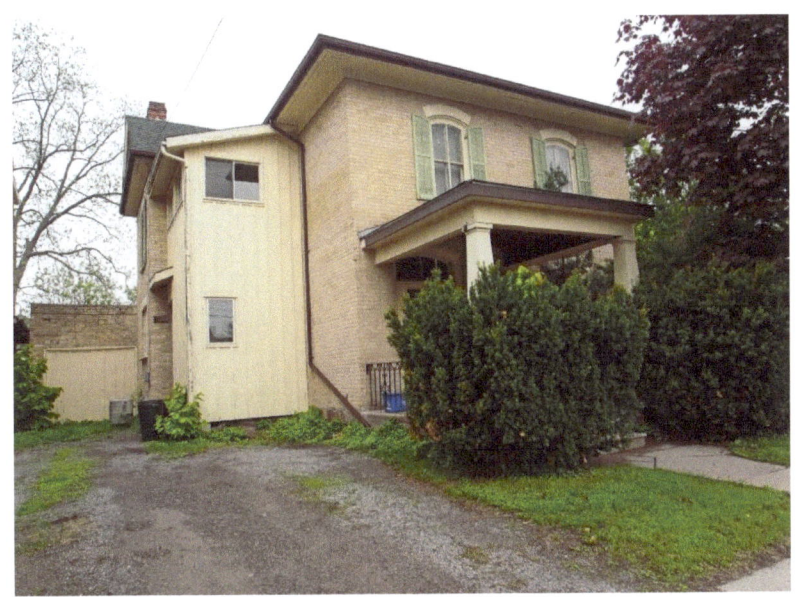

277 Rubidge Street - Italianate

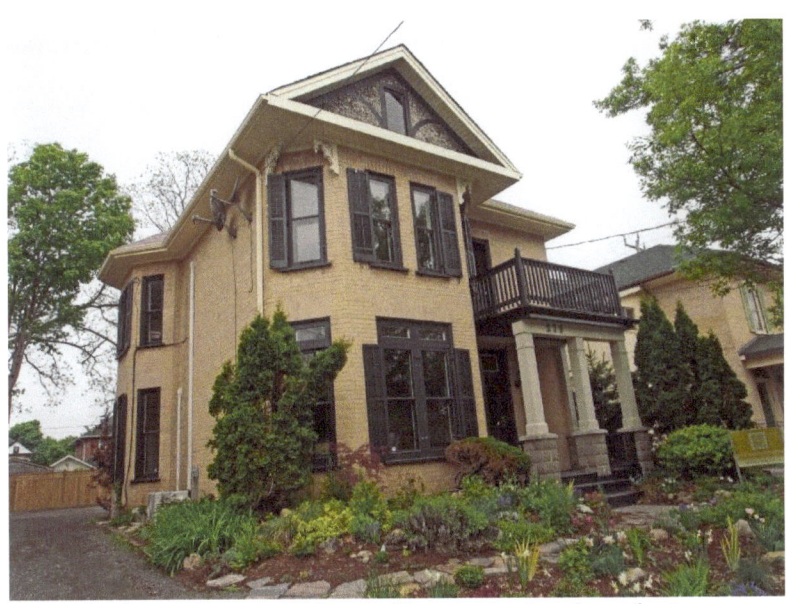

273 Rubidge Street – Edwardian, cornice brackets, second floor balcony

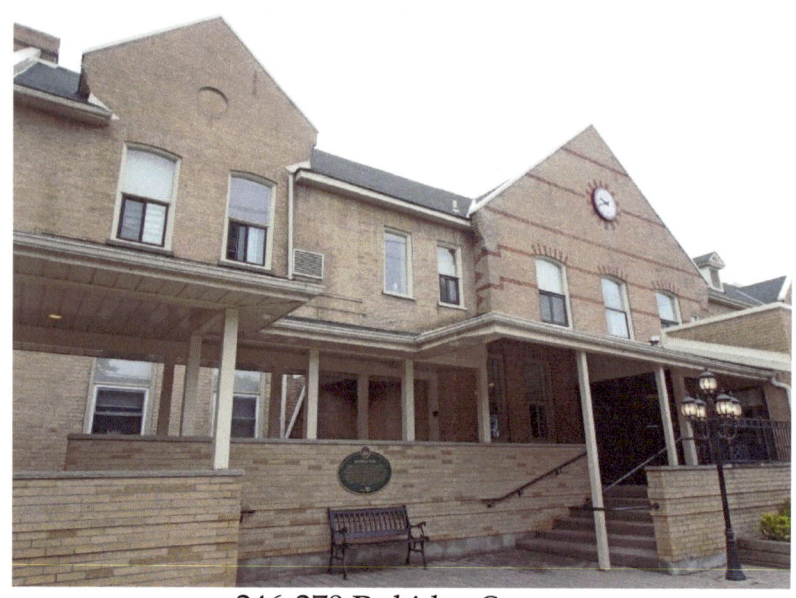

246-270 Rubidge Street
Gothic, dichromatic brick work, banding

On October 17, 1964, Rubidge Hall was opened by Governor General Georges Vanier as the first site of Trent University. It was named after Captain Charles Rubidge (1787-1873), a prominent land agent who encouraged settlement in Peterborough County. Originally built as the South Central School, the Victorian building had fallen into disrepair by the mid-twentieth century. In 1963 the hall was purchased by the newly-incorporated university and was renovated. A central lecture hall, seminar rooms, laboratories for the sciences, and offices for the president, registrar and faculty were included. The university's rapid growth downtown, and at the Nassau Mills' site, resulted in the hall's closure in 1973. Renovated again in the 1990s, the hall is now Rubidge Retirement Residence.

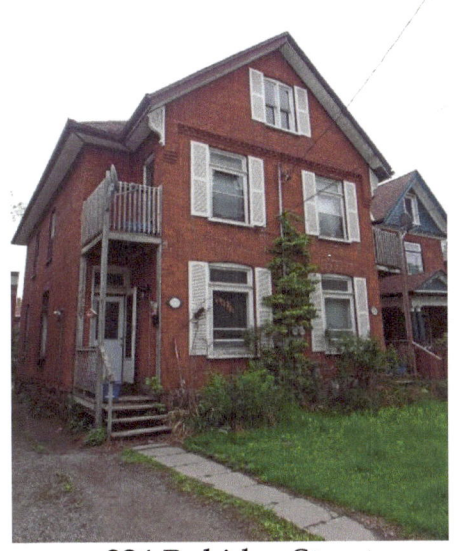

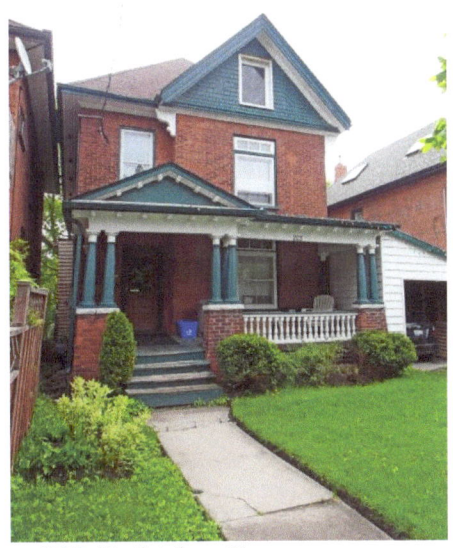

224 Rubidge Street
Gothic Revival
Second floor balcony on side

222 Rubidge Street
Edwardian, Doric pillars,
pediment above verandah

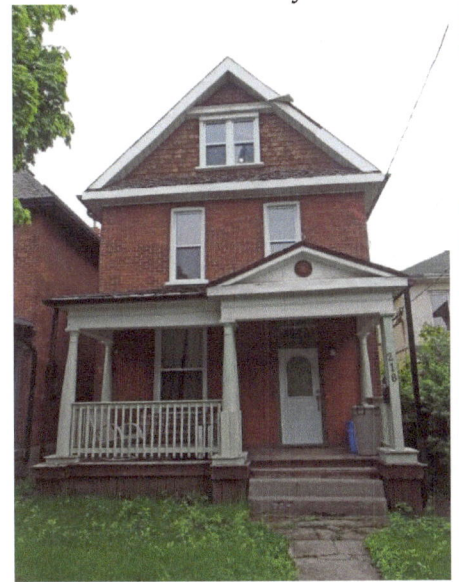

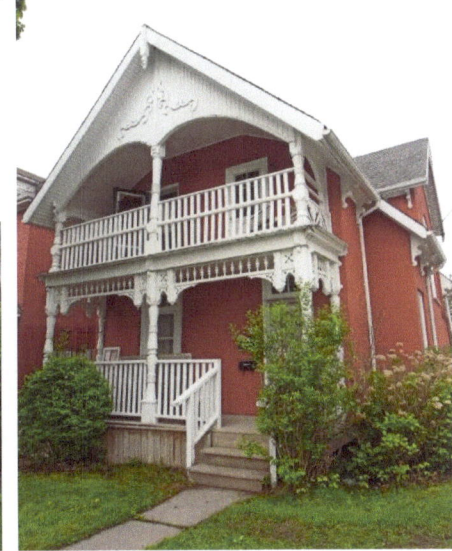

218 Rubidge Street
Edwardian, pediment

corner Wolfe and Rubidge Street
finial on gable, 2nd floor balcony

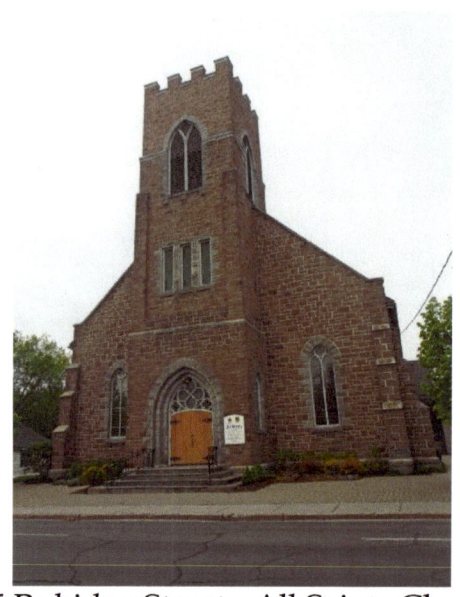

235 Rubidge Street - All Saints Church

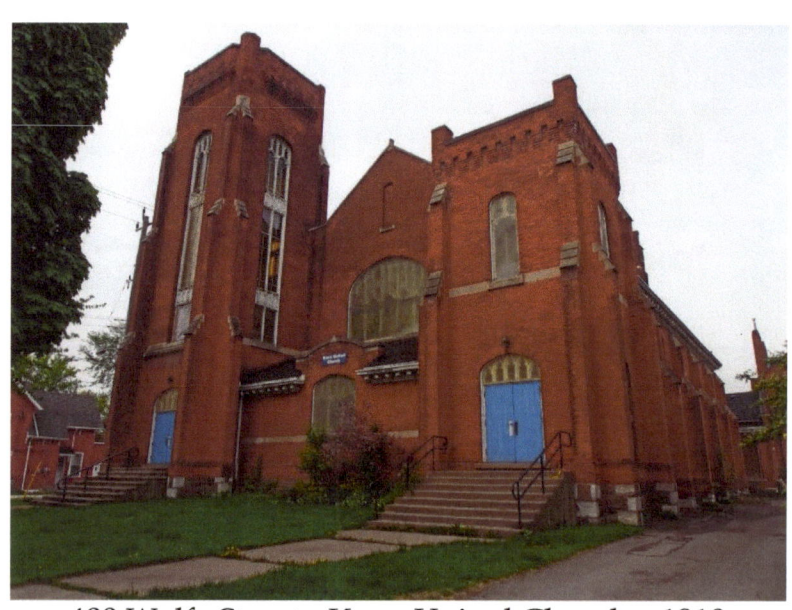

400 Wolfe Street - Knox United Church – 1910

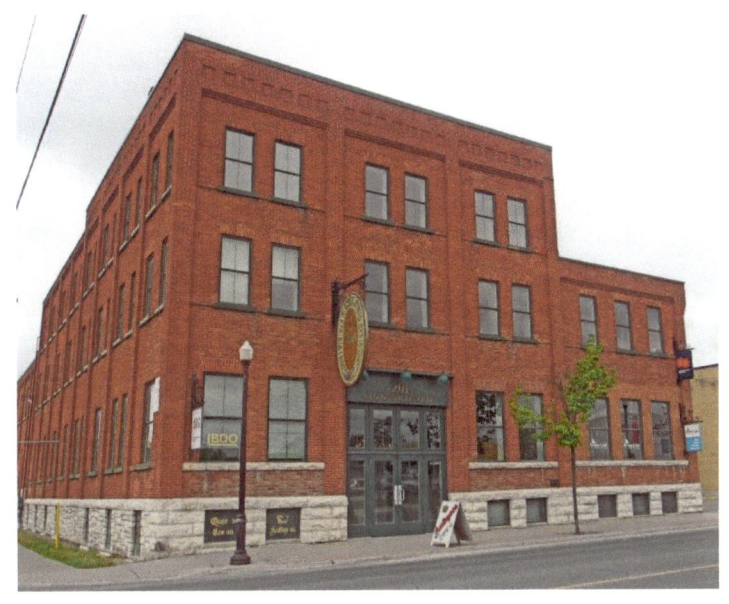

Harness Factory 1897-1997, 201 George Street North

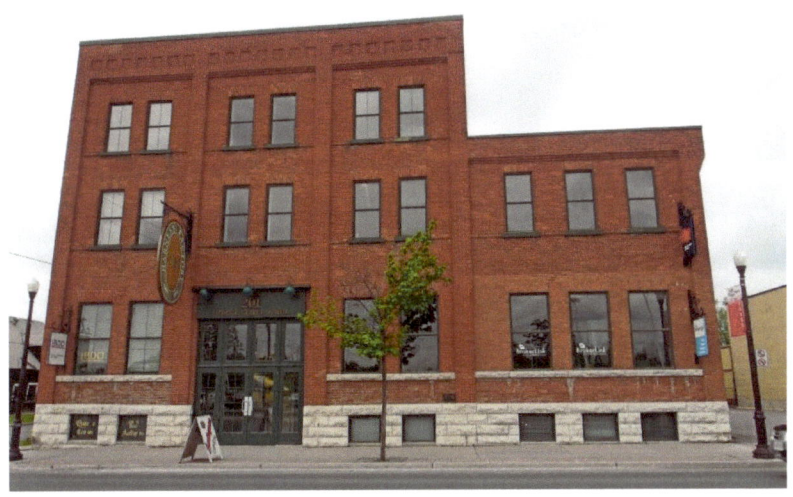

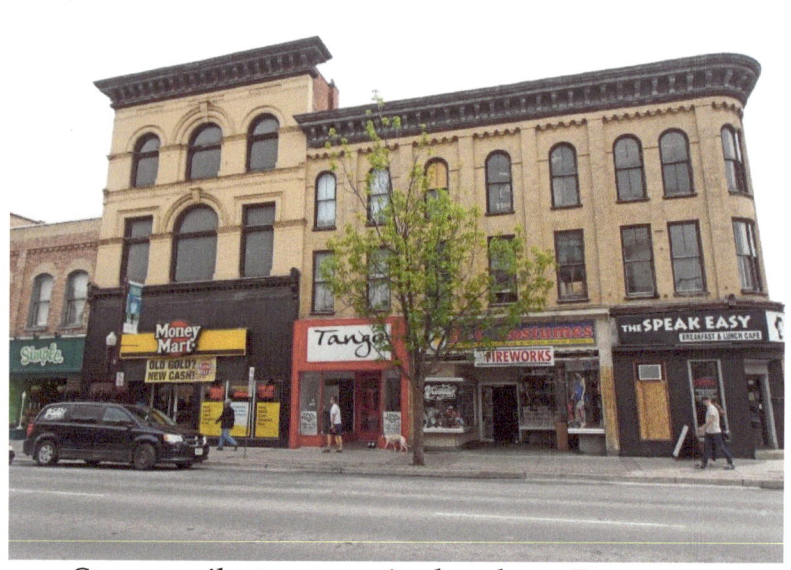

George Street – pilasters, cornice brackets, Romanesque style voussoirs with keystones building on left

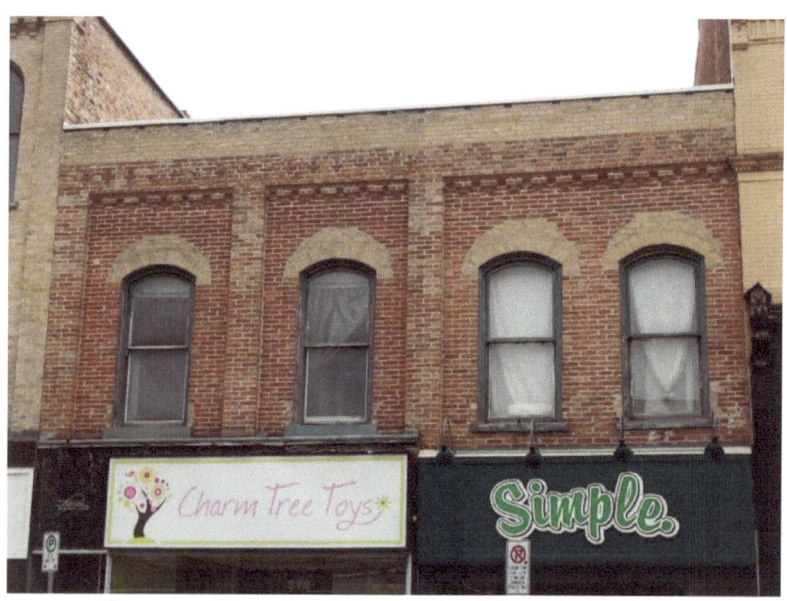

George Street - dentil moulding, pilasters

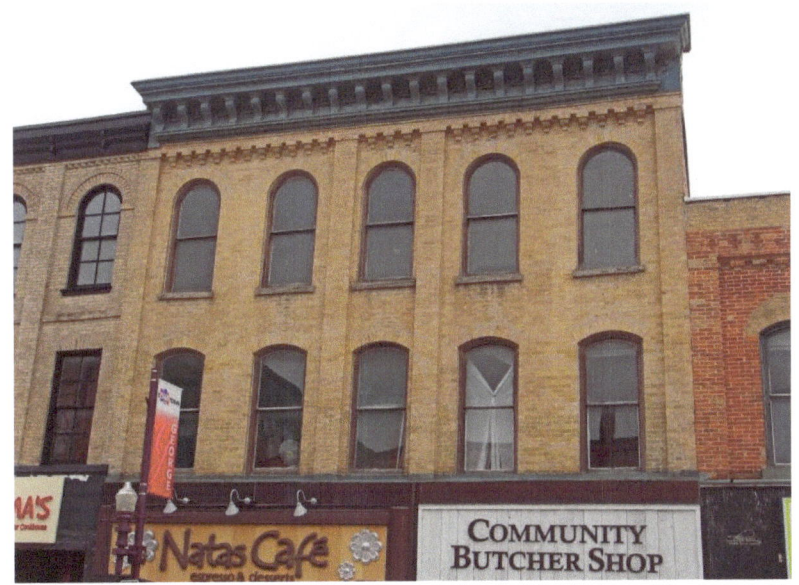

George Street – cornice brackets, bevelled dentil moulding

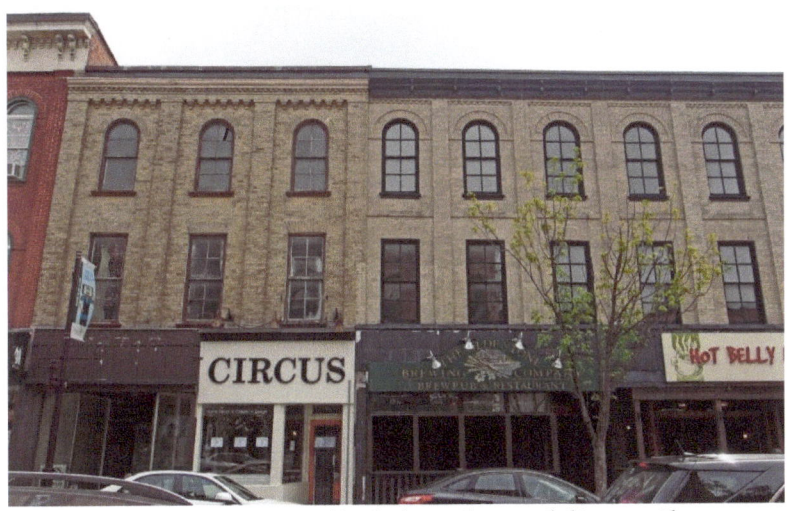

George Street – bevelled dentil moulding, pilasters

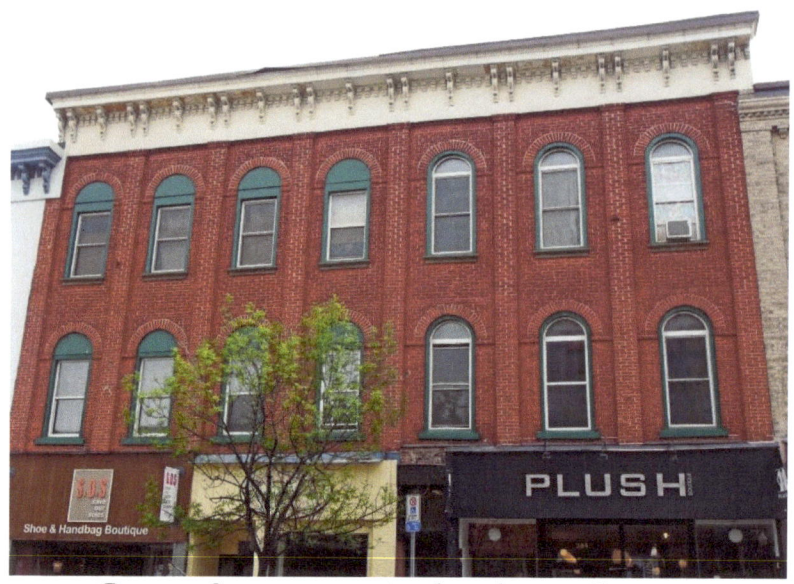

George Street – cornice brackets, pilasters,
arched window voussoirs

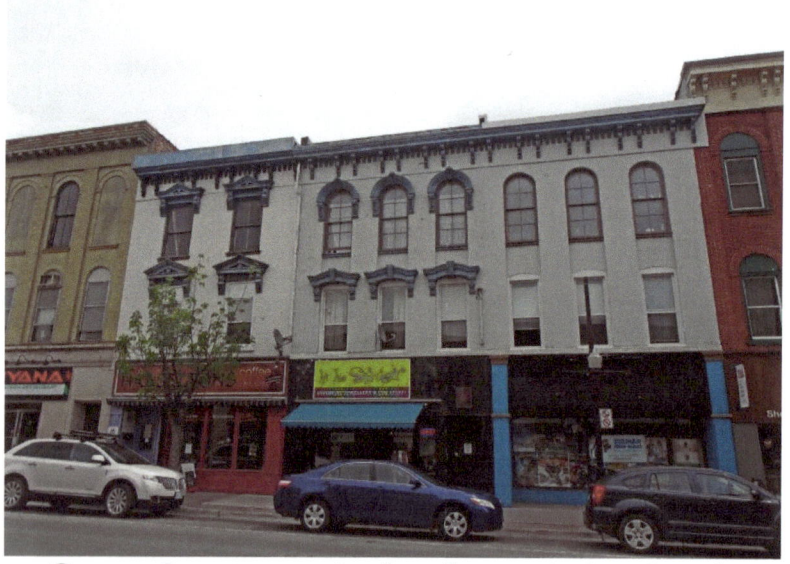

George Street – cornice brackets, window hoods

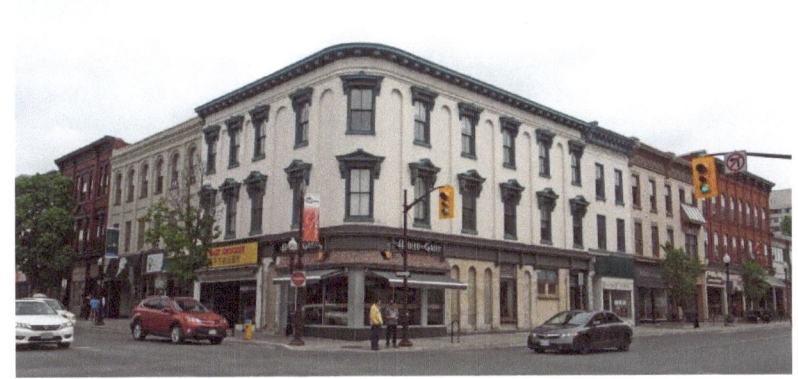

Corner of George and Hunter Streets

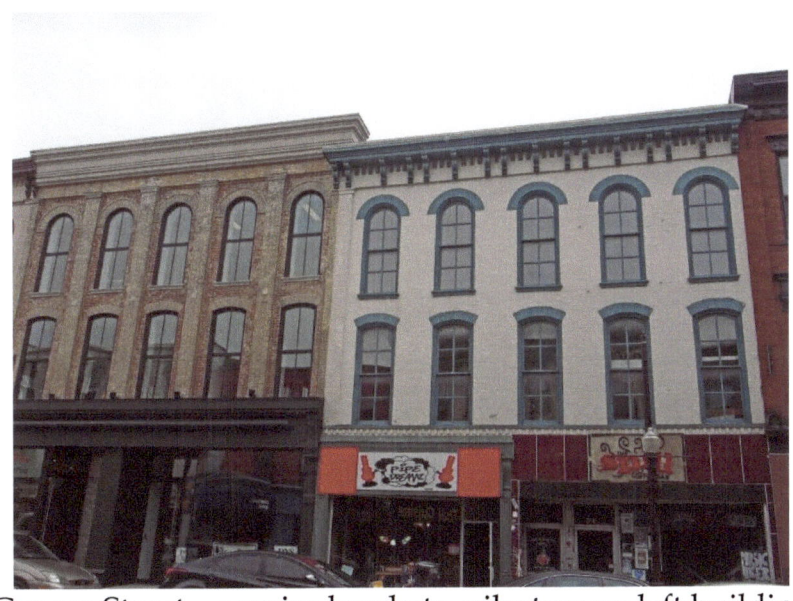

George Street – cornice brackets, pilasters on left building

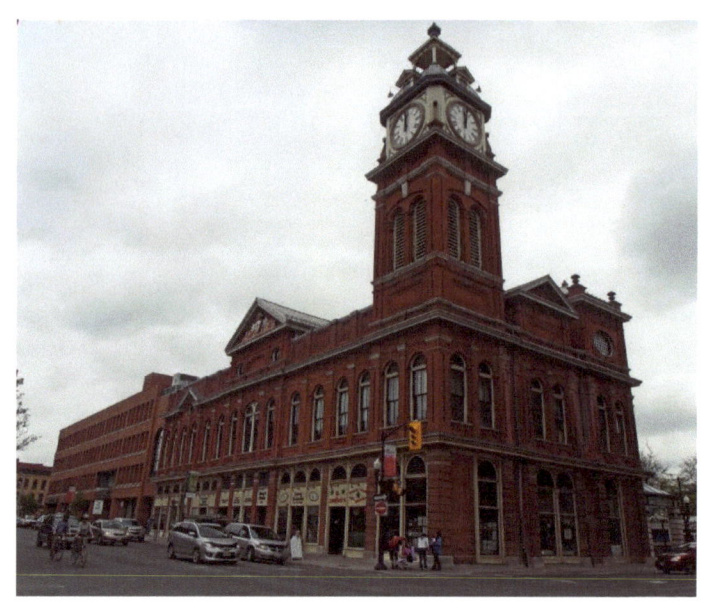

George Street

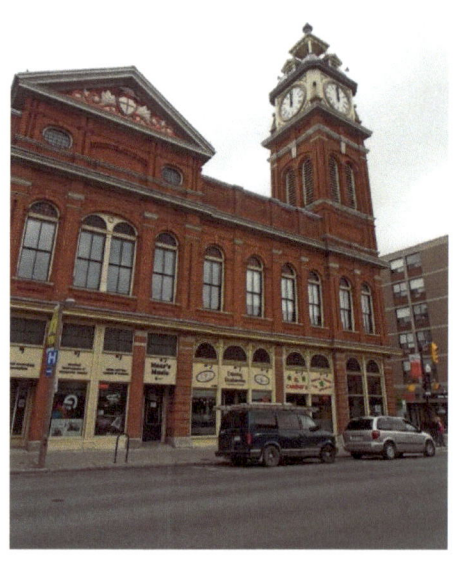

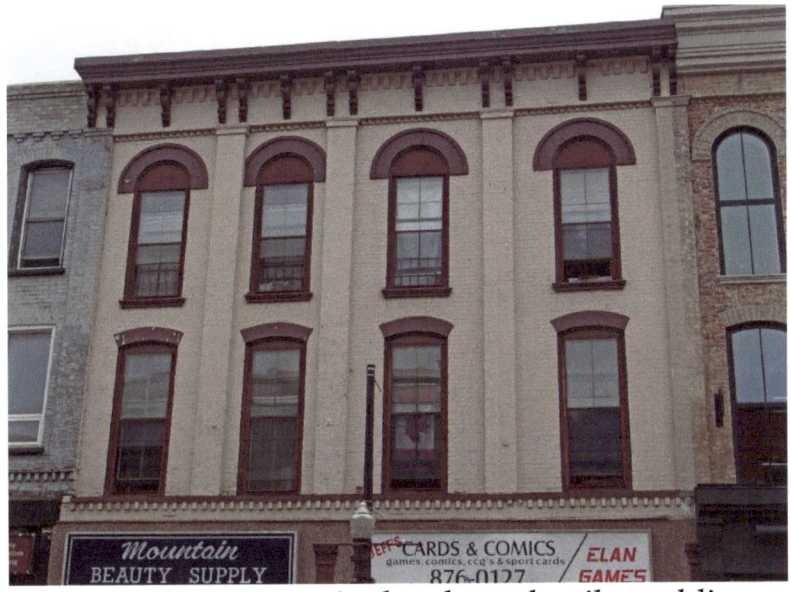

George Street – cornice brackets, dentil moulding

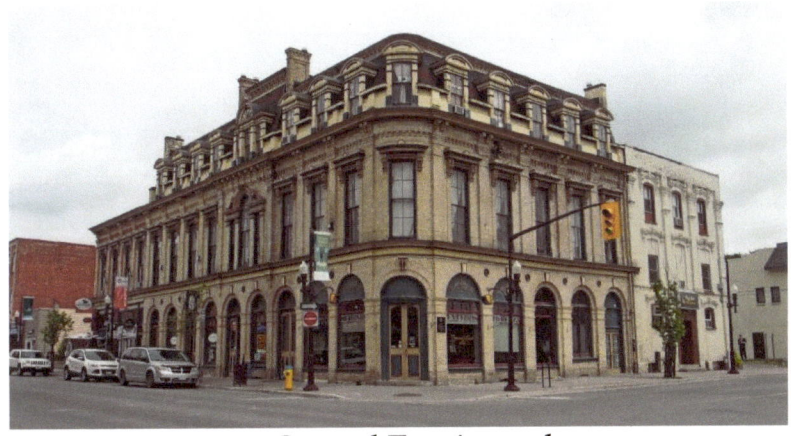

George Street corner – Second Empire style,
window hoods on dormers, banding on top floor;
cornice brackets, dentil moulding, pilasters on 2nd floor;
Romanesque style window voussoirs and keystones
on ground level

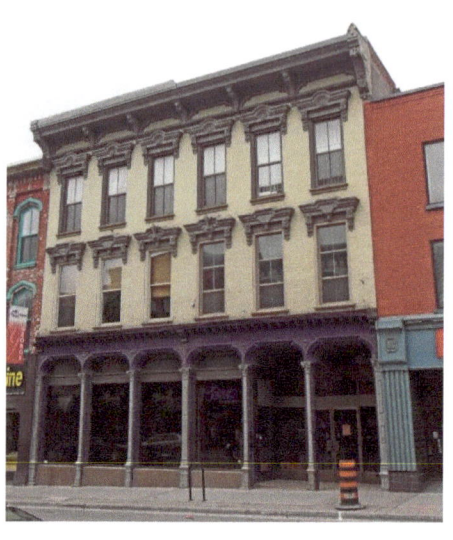

George Street

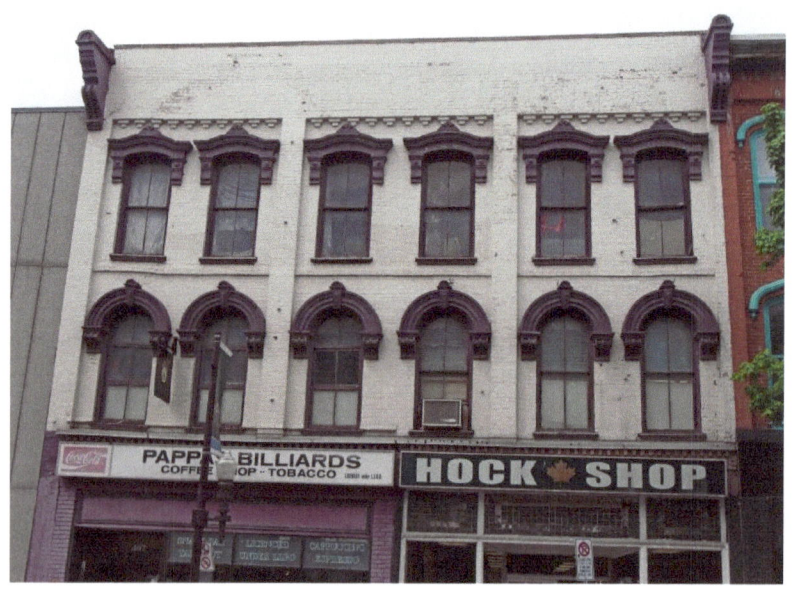

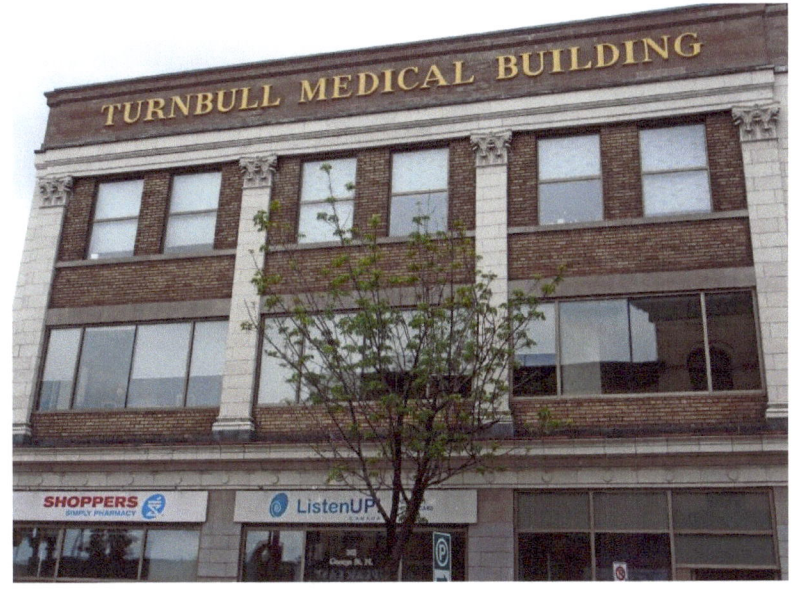

George Street

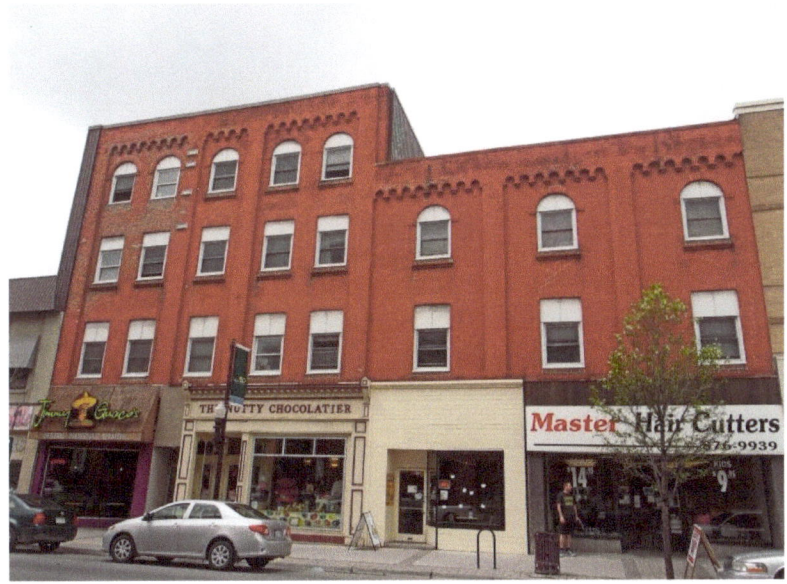

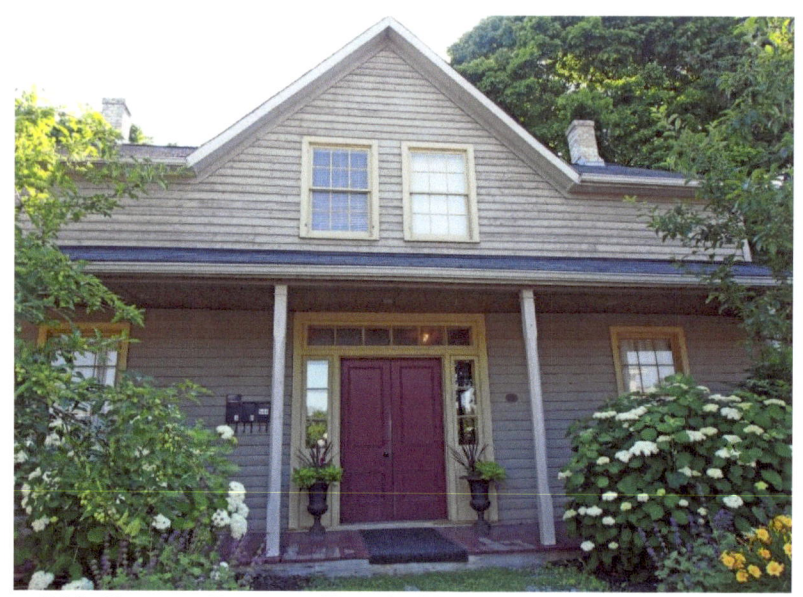

544 George Street – Dr. A. Harvey – cottage c. 1855

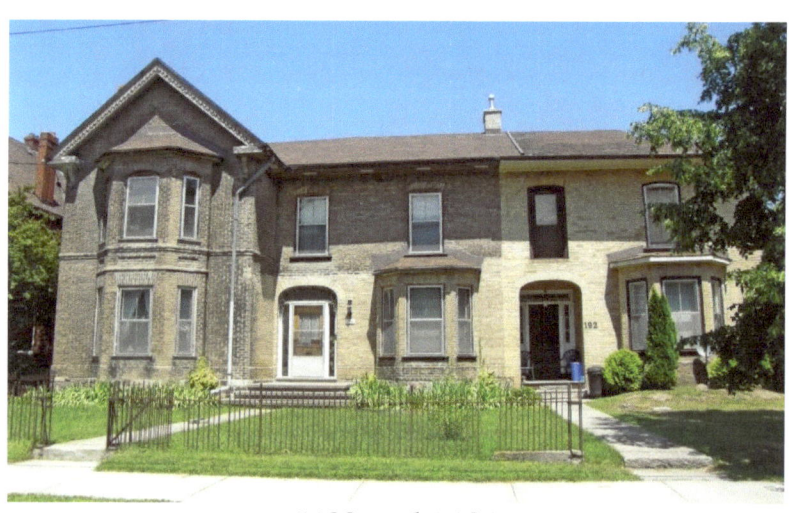

#192 and #194

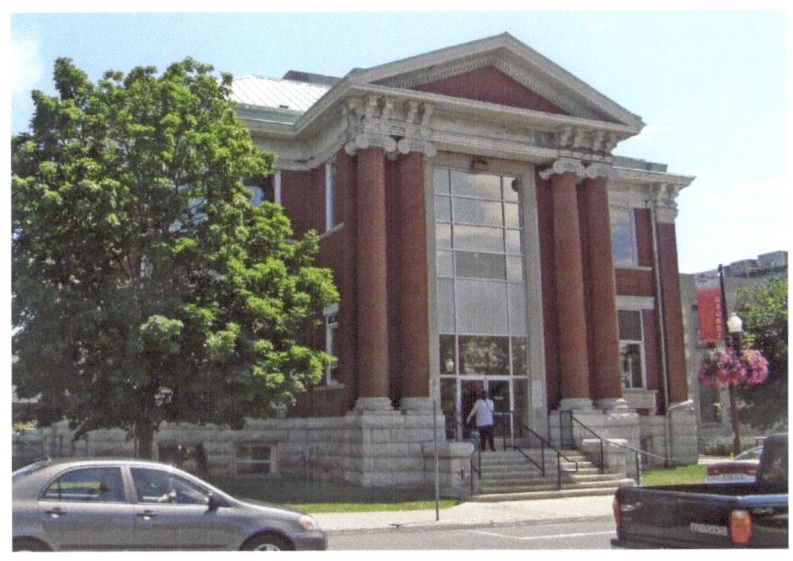

George Street City Hall – Beaux Arts style, cornice brackets, pillars with Ionic capitals, pediment

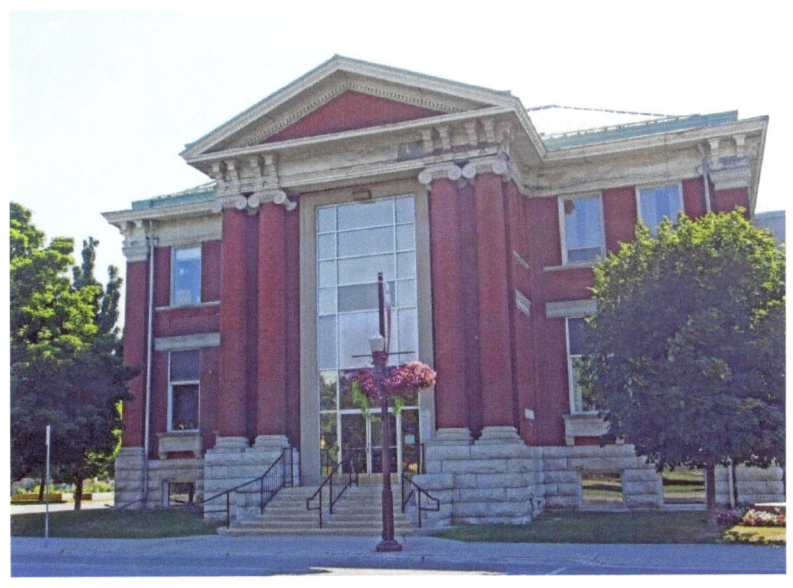

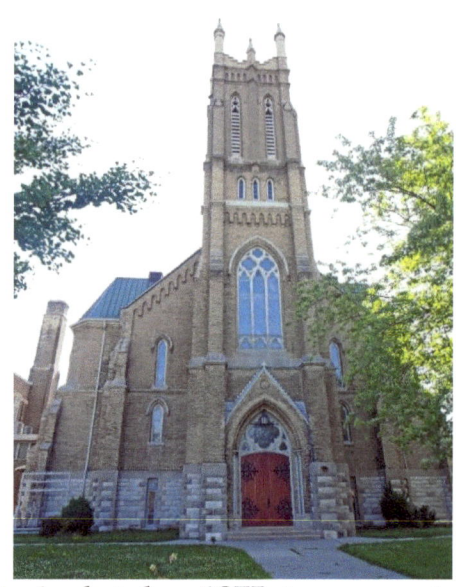

Gothic Revival style – 1875, tower erected in 1891

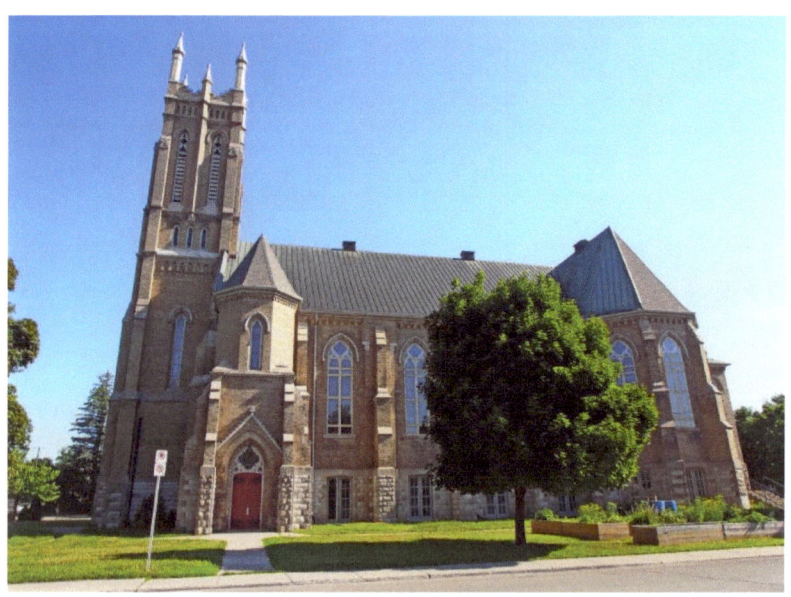

540 George Street - George Street United Church

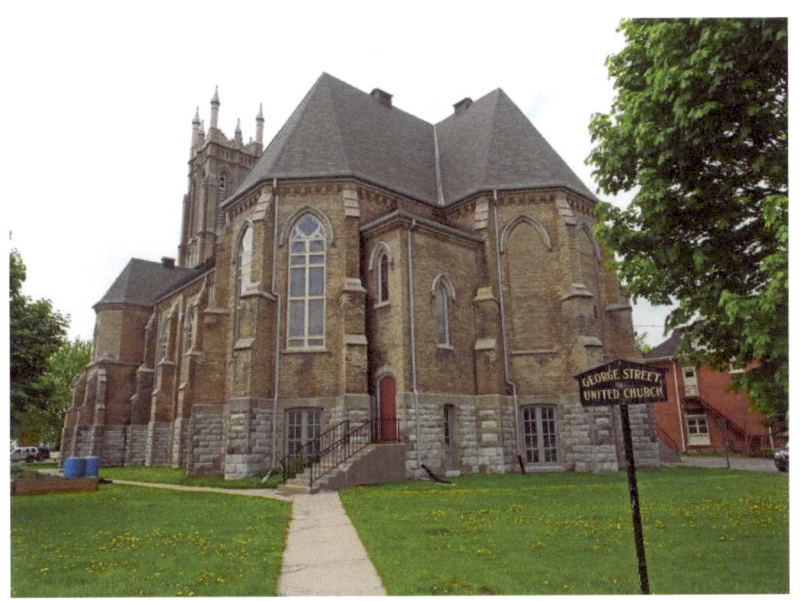

George Street United

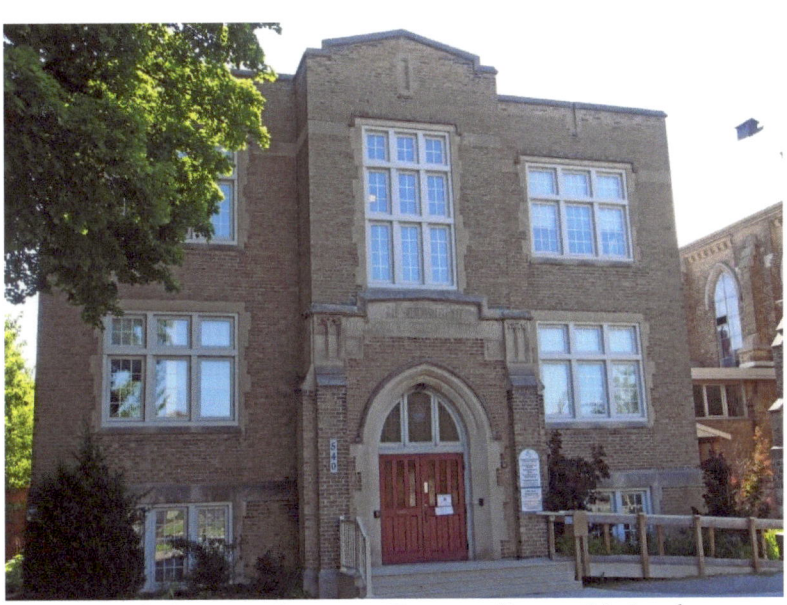

540 George Street - George Street United
Memorial Sunday School

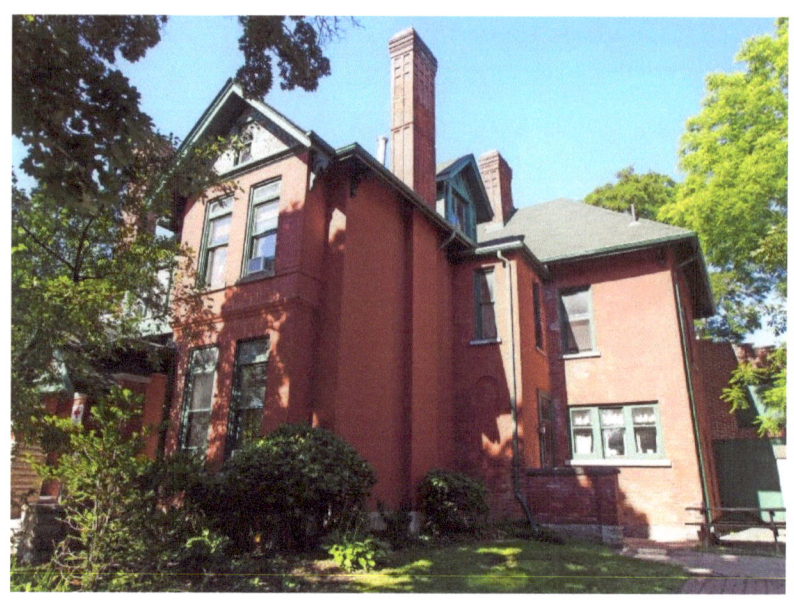

565 George Street – Harstone House 1886 – Queen Anne style
The Harstone family lived here from 1907 to 1982, when the
Red Cross bought the house.

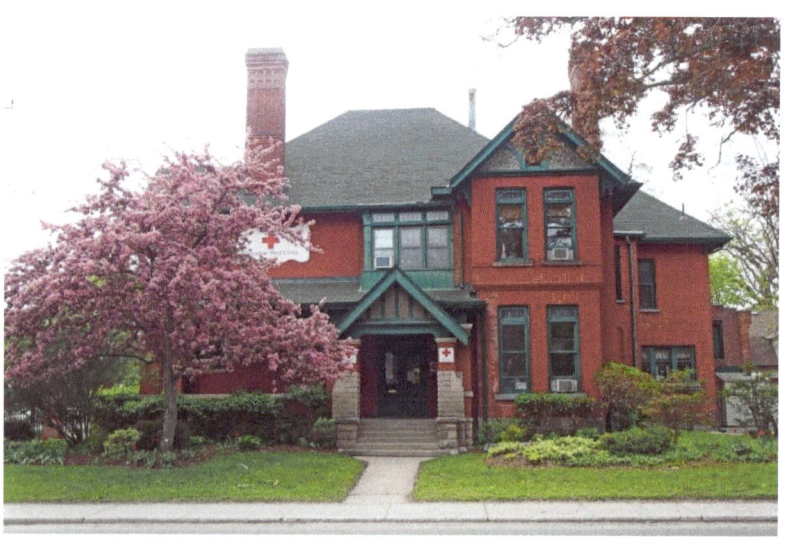

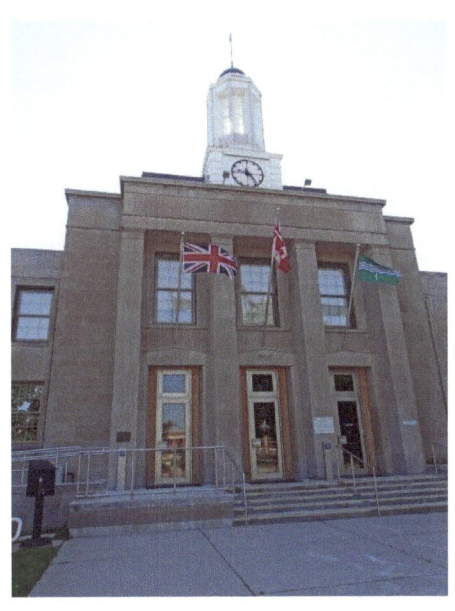

500 George Street – City Hall

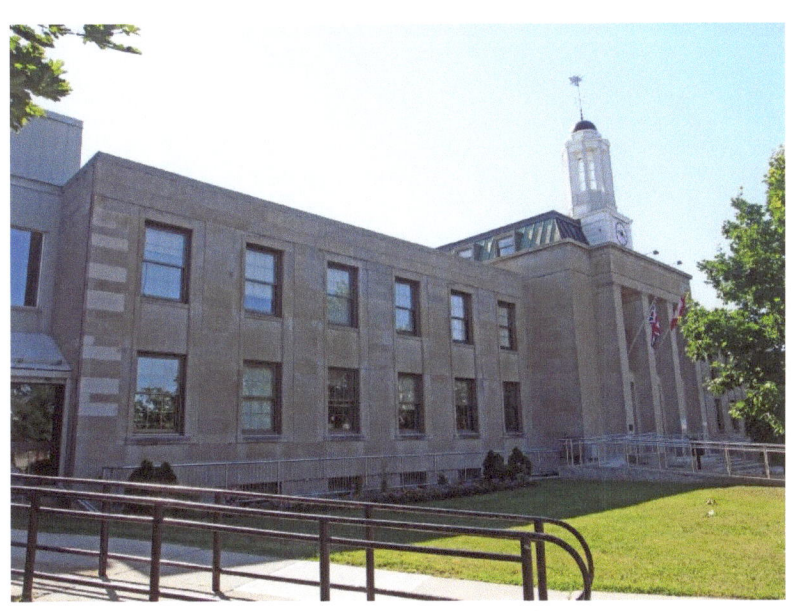

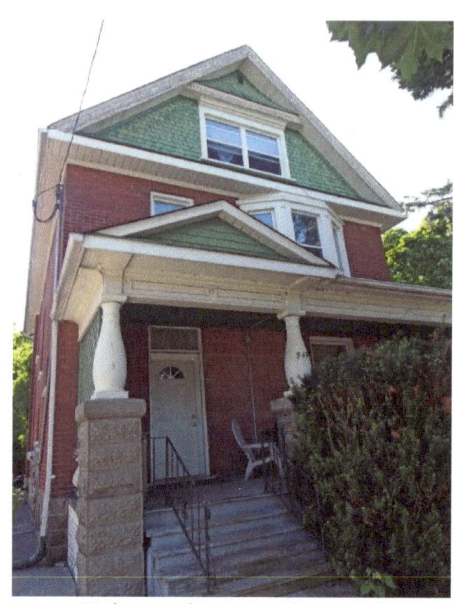

548 George Street – Edwardian style, pediment, bay window

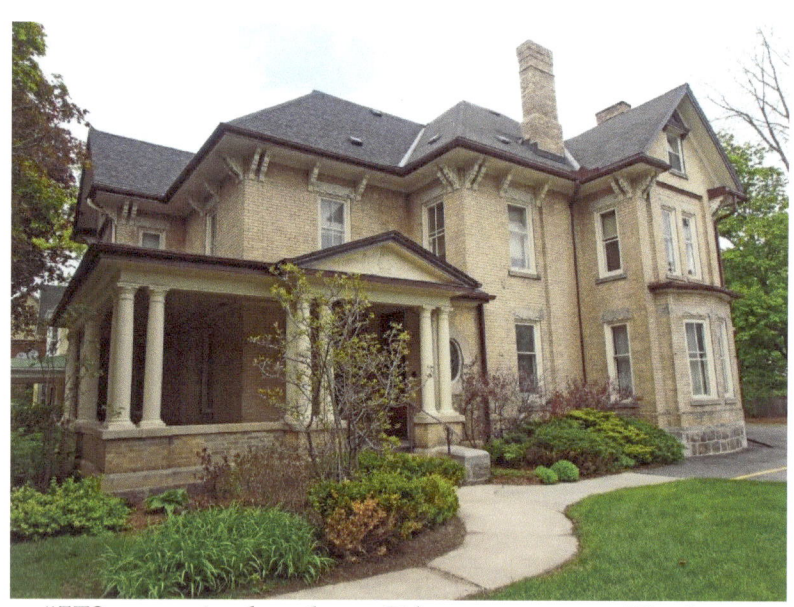

#570 – cornice brackets, 2½ storey tower-like bays,
pediment, doric pillars

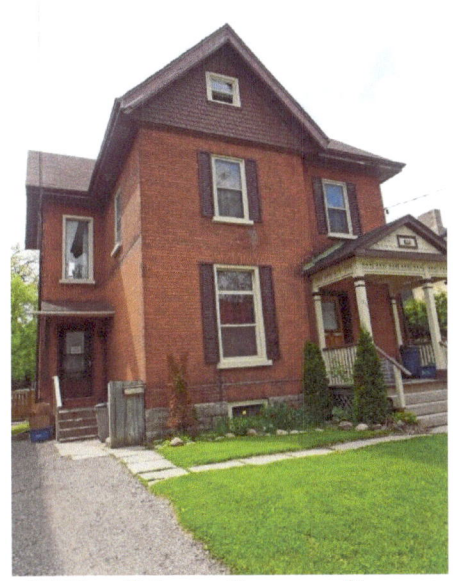

#571 – Edwardian, pediment

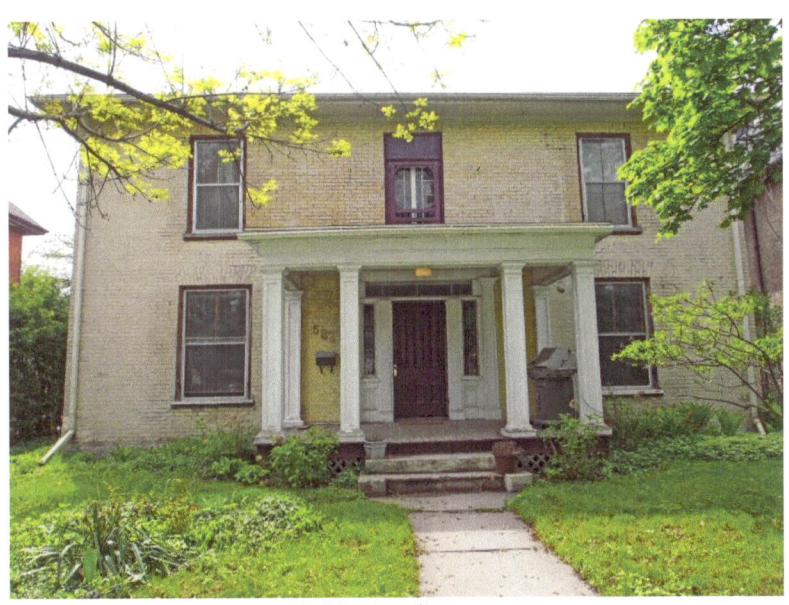

#583 - Italianate

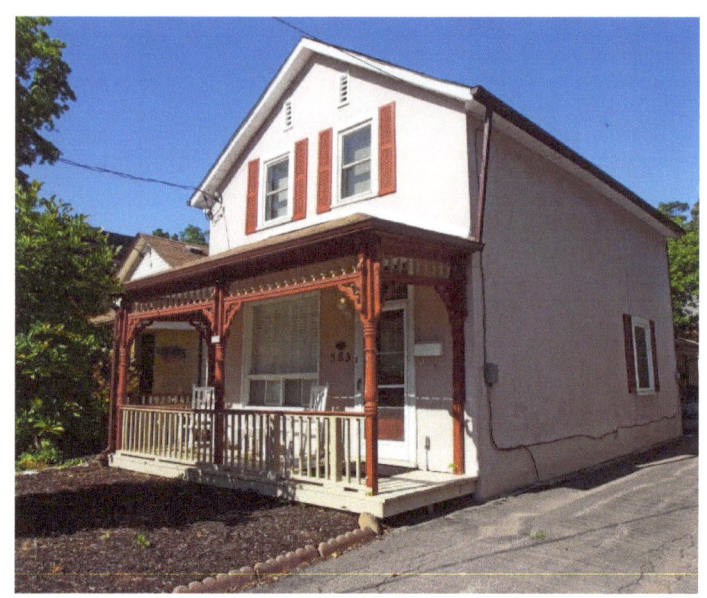

583 Water Street – The William Thornton House 1875
Gothic Revival

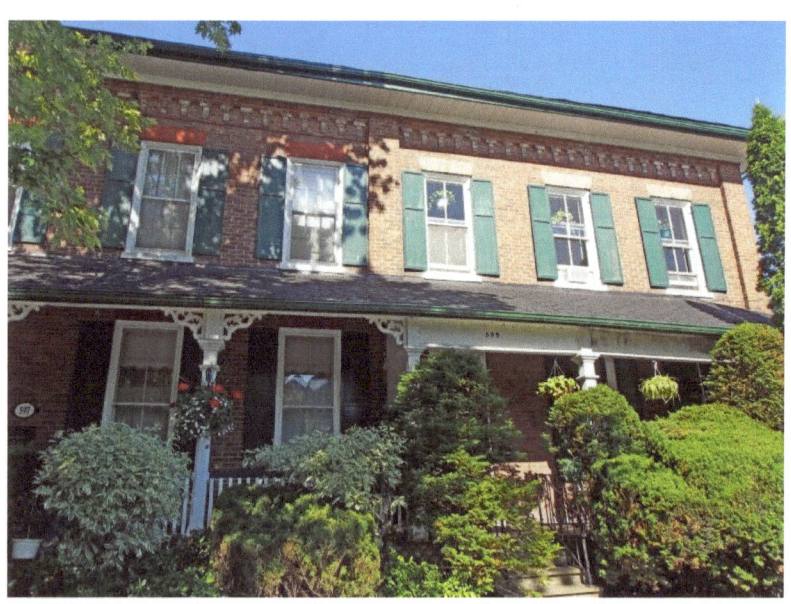

599 Water Street – Georgian style, dentil moulding

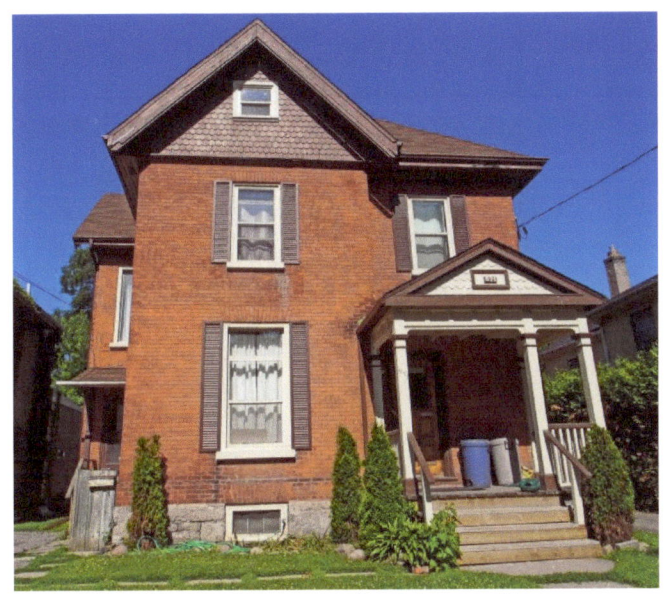

571 Water Street – Gothic, pediment

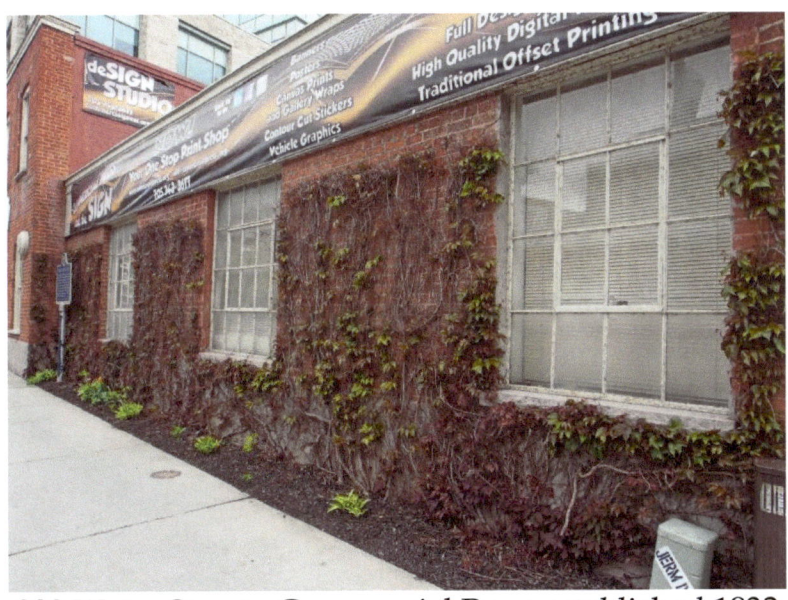

290 Water Street - Commercial Press established 1932

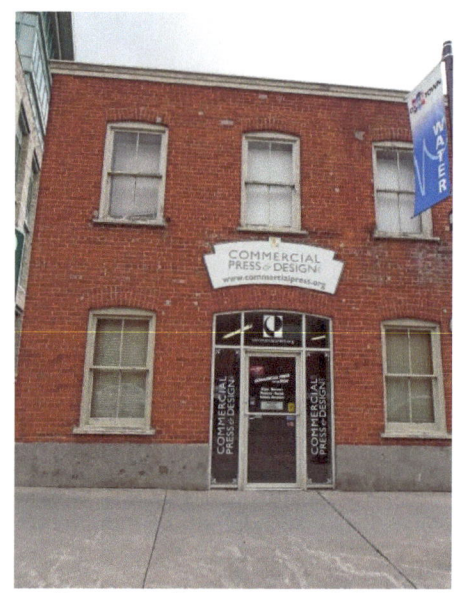

290 Water Street – Commercial Press & Design

Near this site in 1820, the community's first resident, Adam Scott built a saw mill and a gristmill. The small settlement that grew around them was known as Scott's Plains until 1826 when it was renamed in honour of Peter Robinson. Although of primitive construction, the mills were of great benefit to the early settlers including the Irish immigrants brought over by Robinson in 1825. Scott relinquished possession of the mills in 1827 and in 1835 they were destroyed by fire.

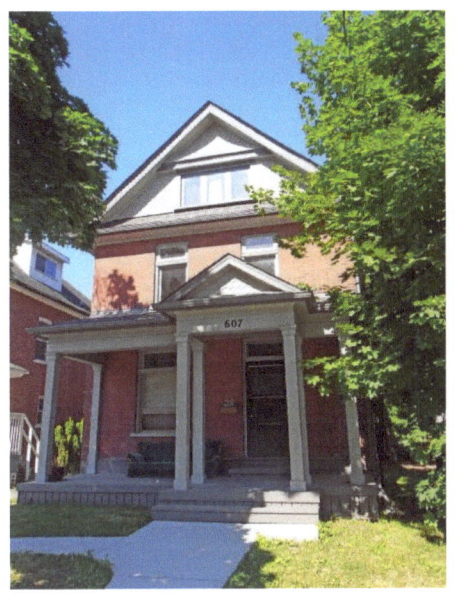

607 Water Street
Pediment, Gothic

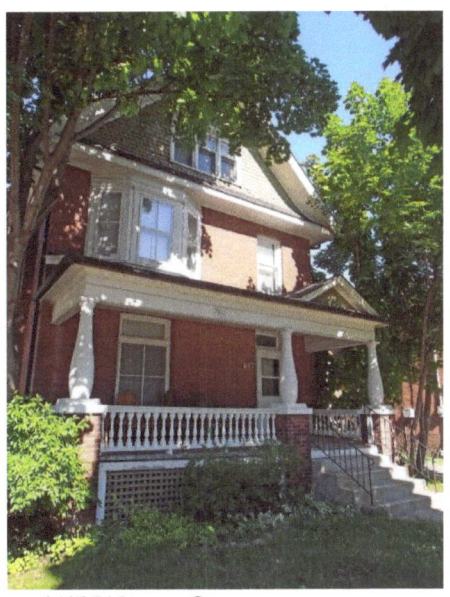

617 Water Street
Gothic

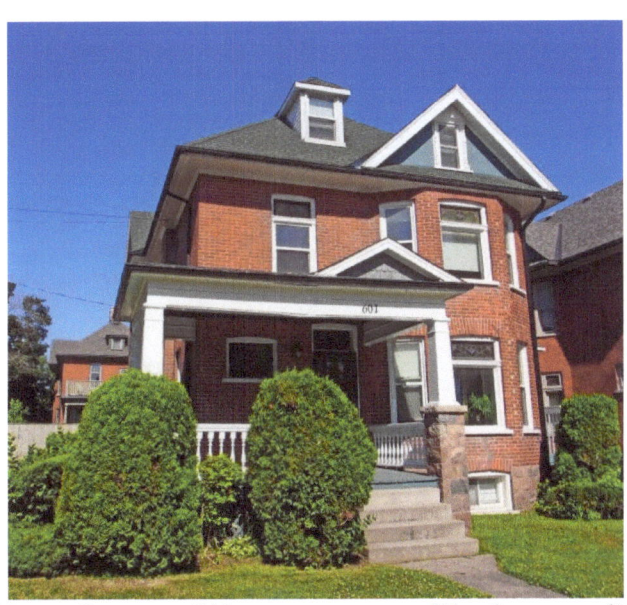

601 Water Street – 2½ storey tower-like bay, pediment,
dormer in attic

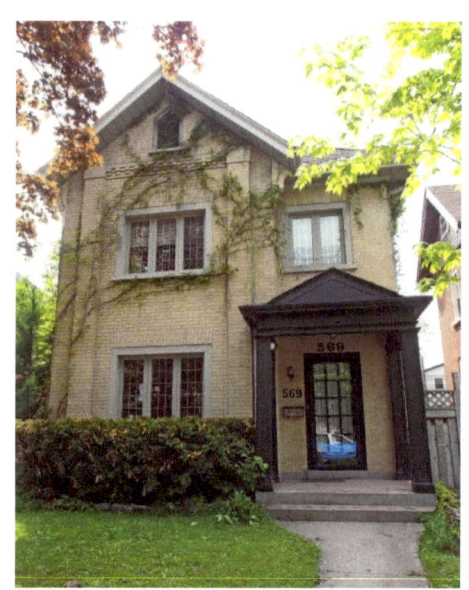

569 Water Street – Gothic, pediment

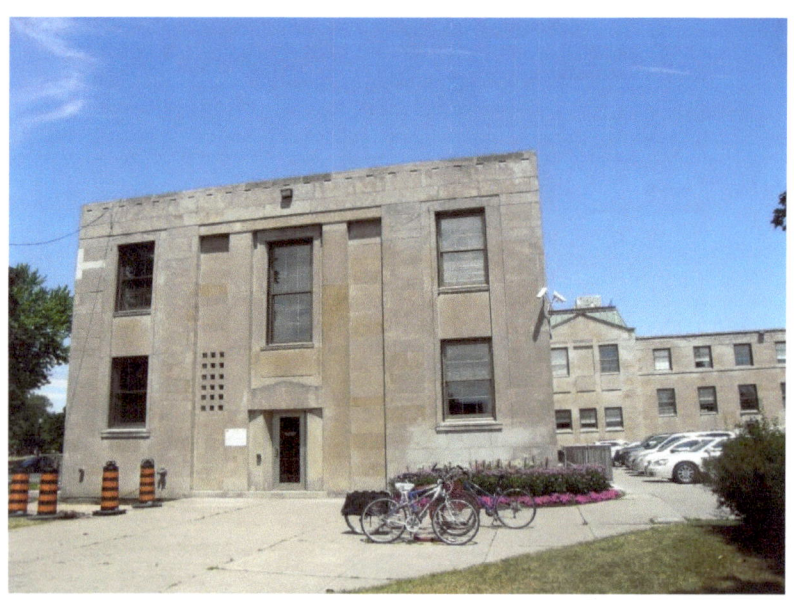

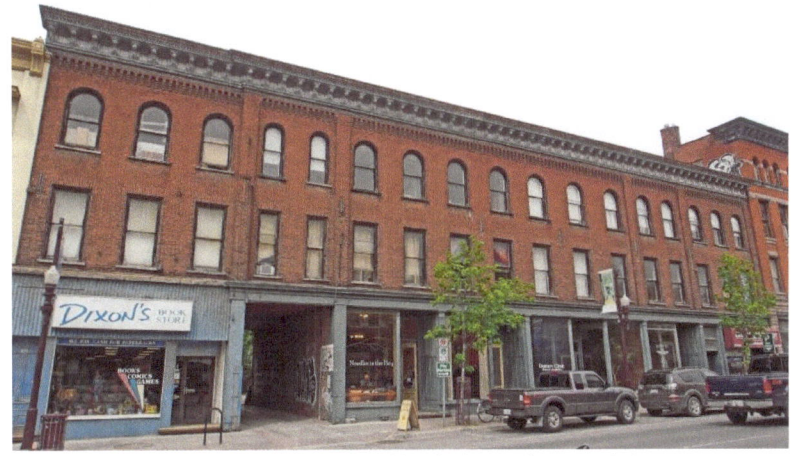

Water Street - bevelled dentil moulding

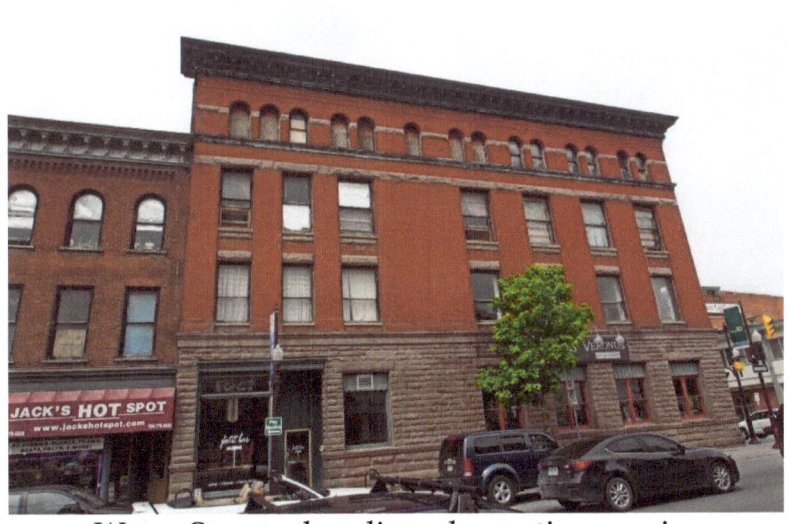

Water Street – banding, decorative cornice

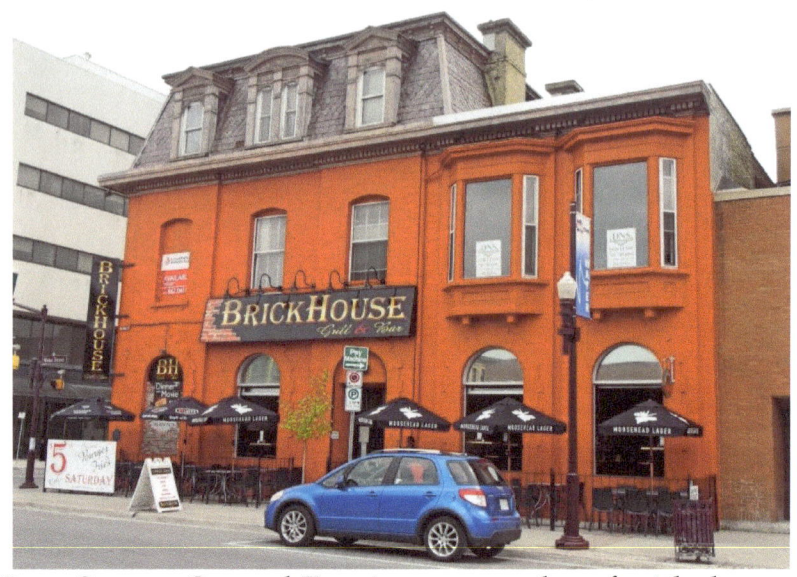

Water Street – Second Empire, mansard roof with dormers

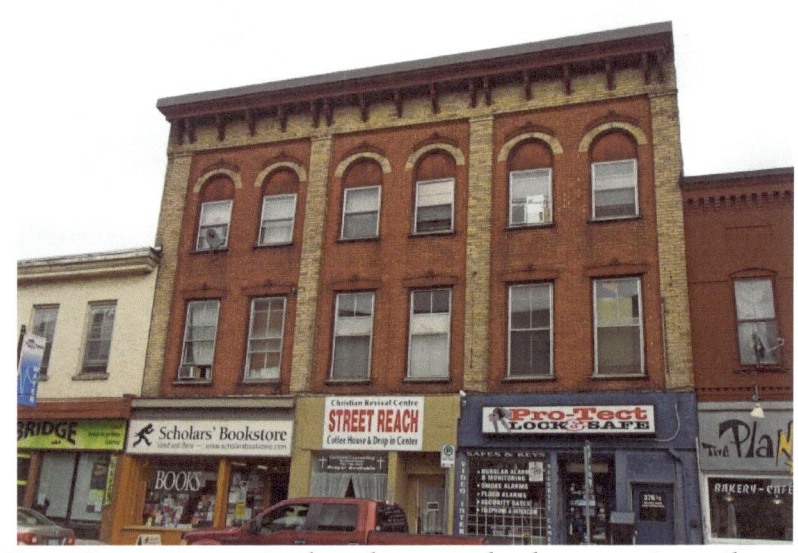

Water Street – cornice brackets, arched voussoirs, pilasters

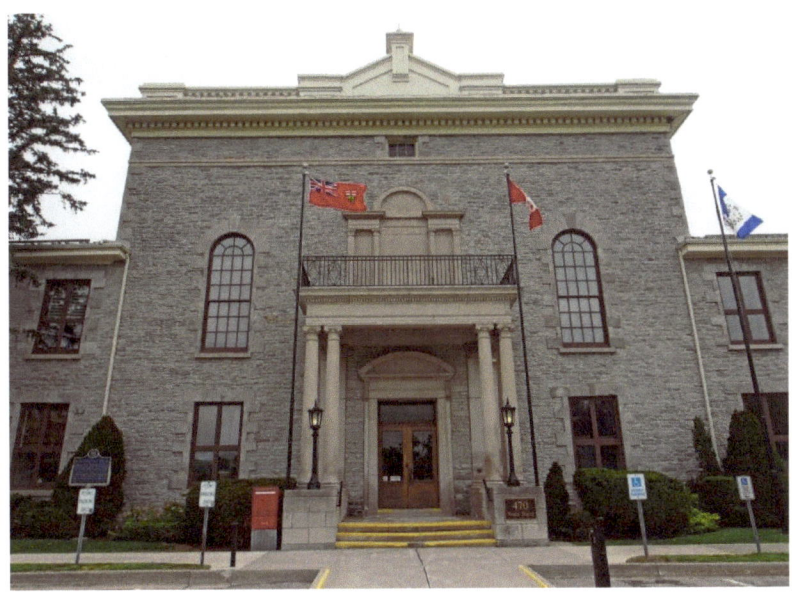

In 1838 the District of Colborne was created and Peterborough was chosen as the district town. In June of that year, the district magistrates authorized the construction of a court house and jail. The court house was completed in 1840 and the jail in 1842 with stone quarried from Jackson's Park.

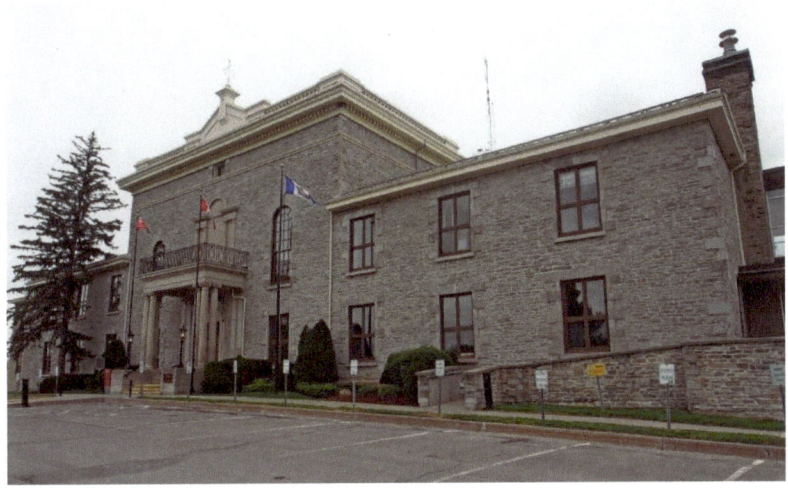

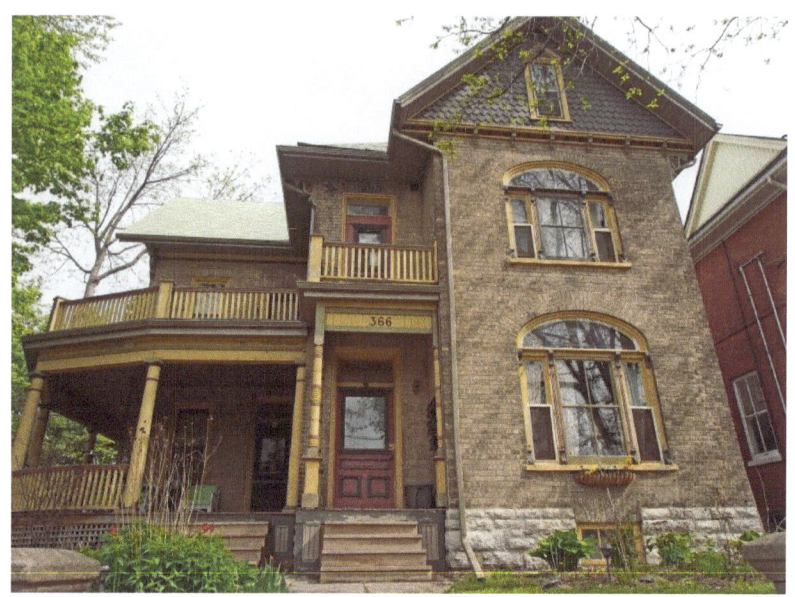

366 Simcoe Street – Edwardian, cornice brackets, 2nd floor balcony and verandah

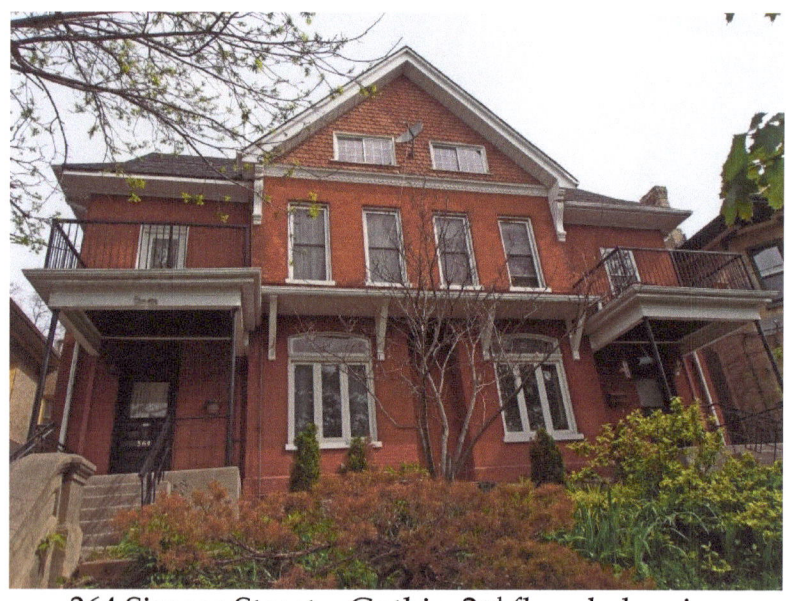

364 Simcoe Street – Gothic, 2nd floor balconies

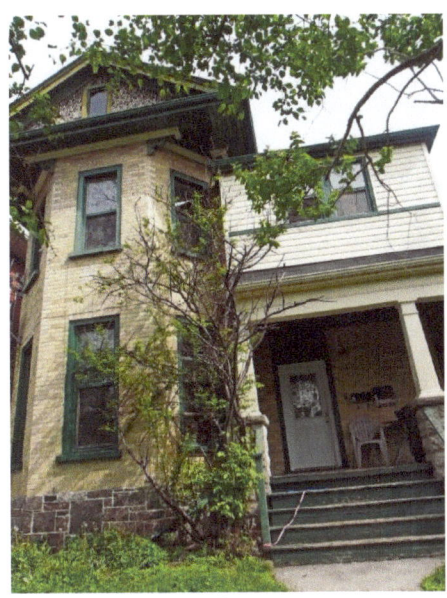 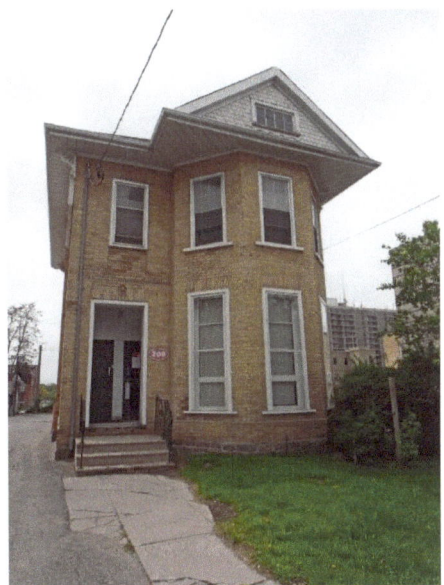

Simcoe Street              209 Simcoe Street

2½ storey tower-like bay

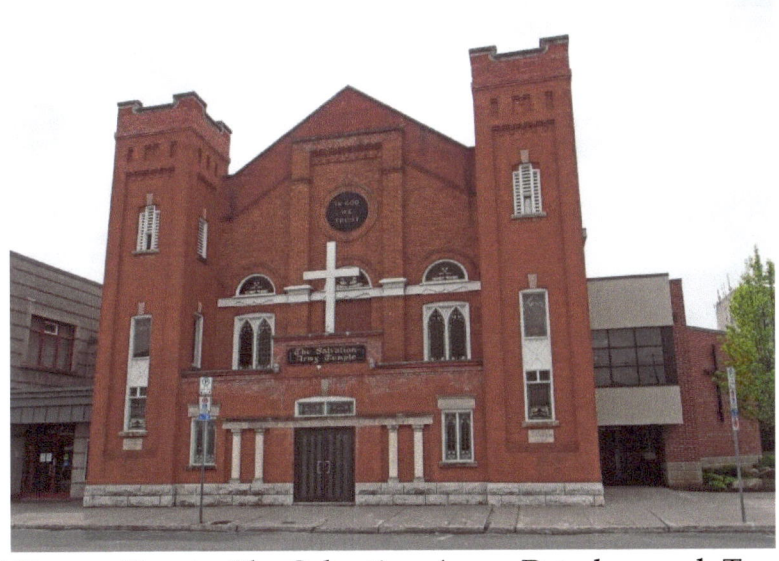

219 Simcoe Street - The Salvation Army Peterborough Temple
erected 1888 – bevelled dentil moulding, pilasters

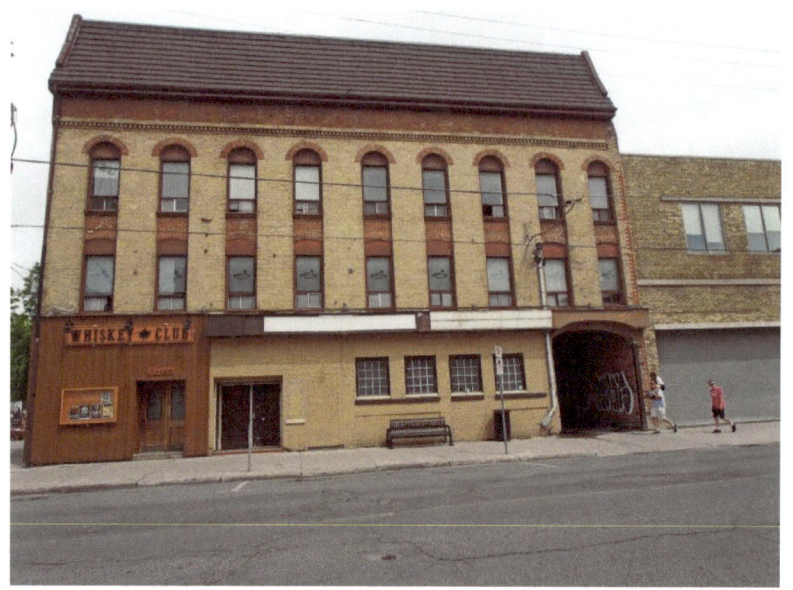

Simcoe Street – dentil moulding, dichromatic brickwork

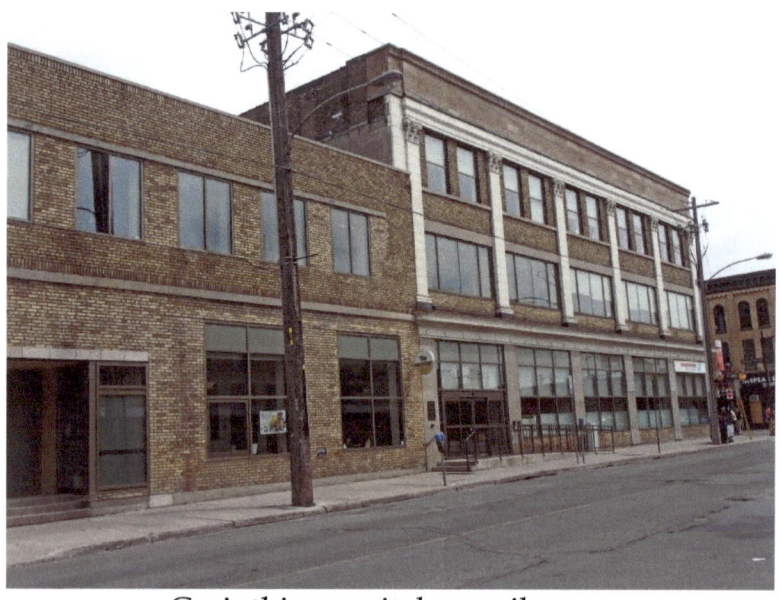

Corinthian capitals on pilasters

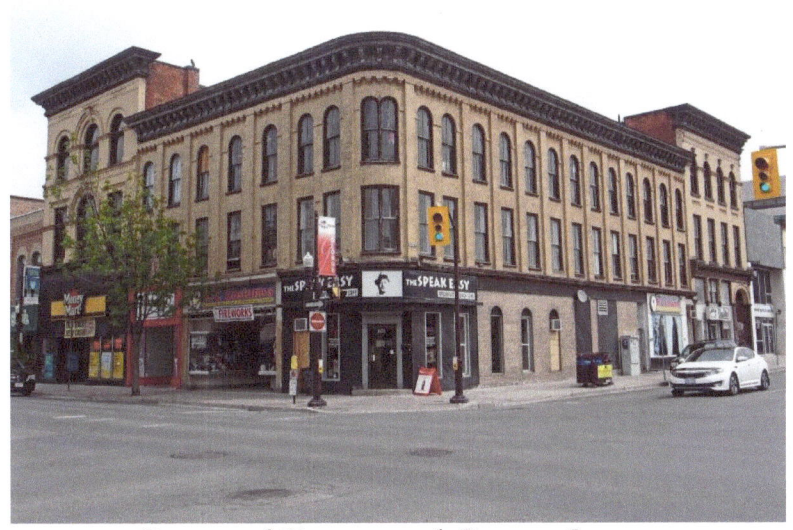

Corner of Simcoe and George Streets
Cornice brackets, bevelled dentil moulding

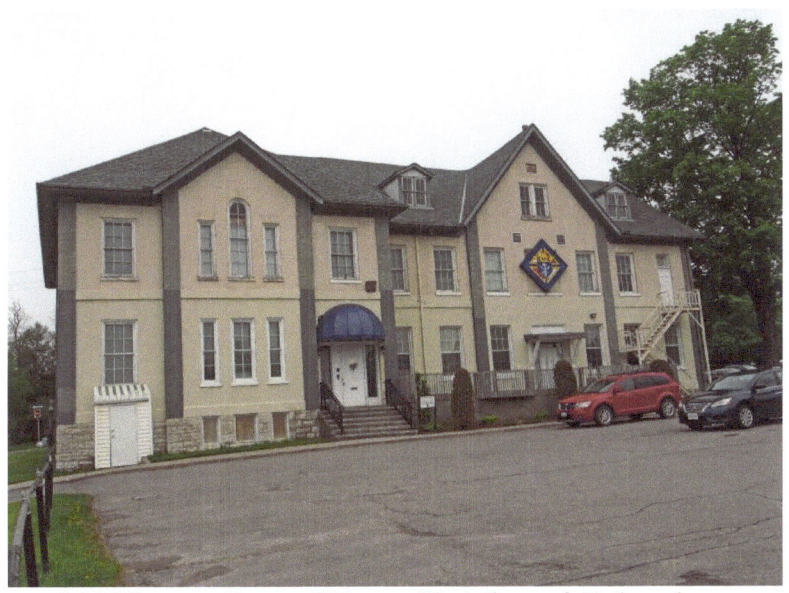

317 Hunter Street West – Knights of Columbus,
dormers in attic

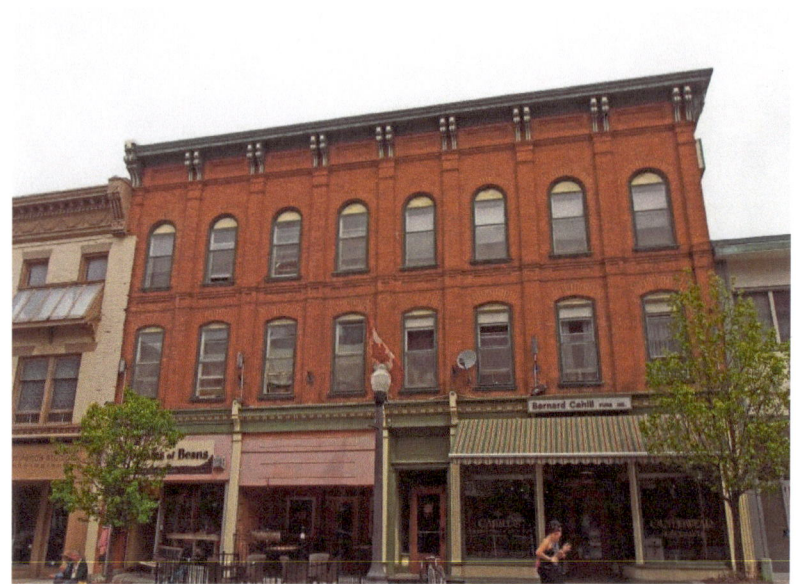

Hunter Street West – cornice brackets, pilasters

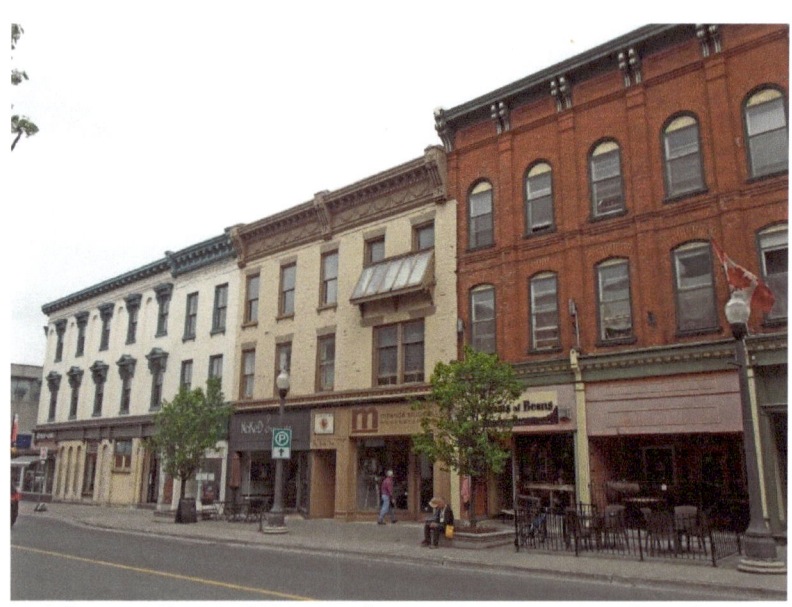

Hunter Street West – decorative cornice, brackets

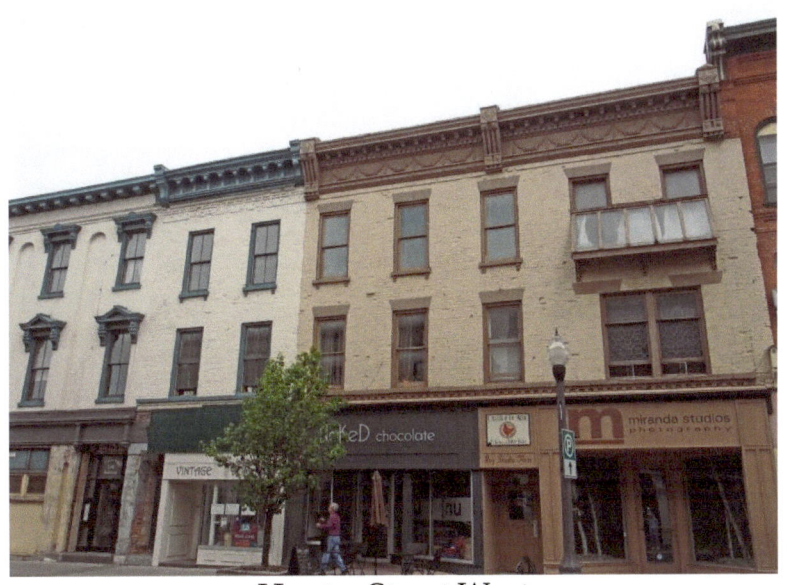

Hunter Street West

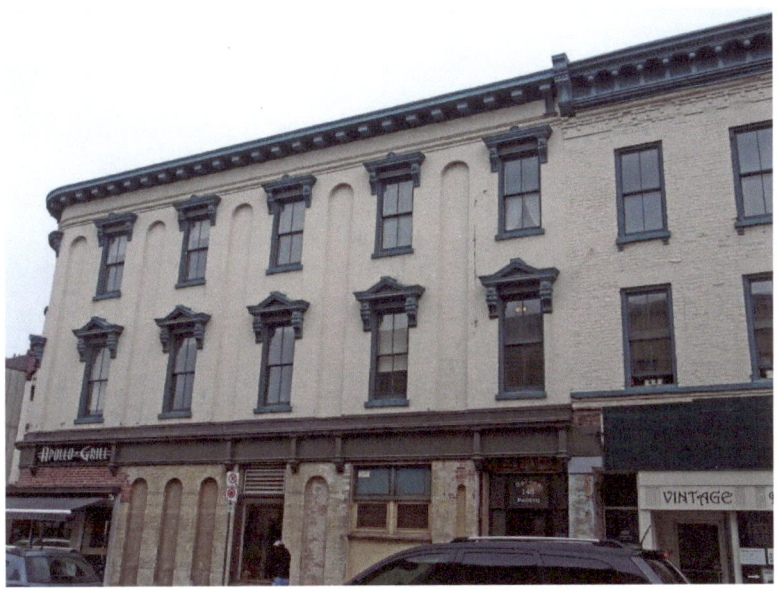

Hunter Street West – window hoods

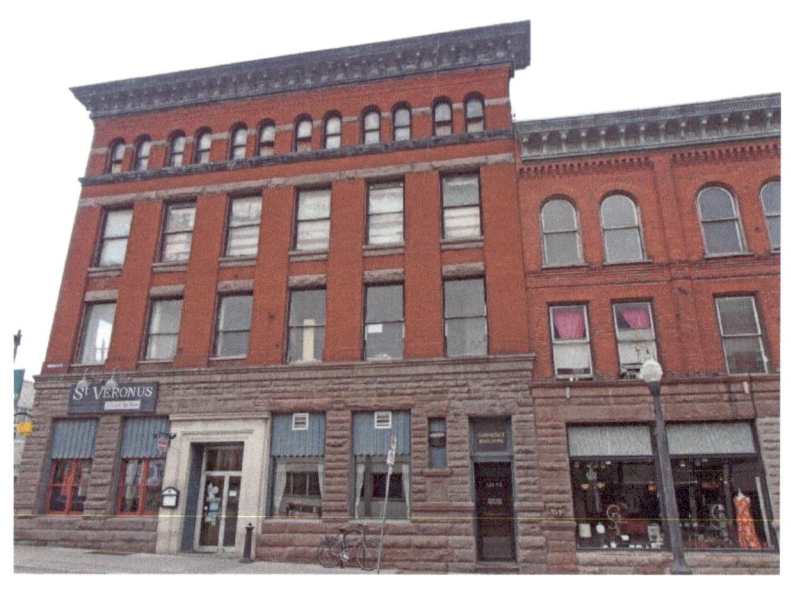

Hunter Street West – banding, cornice brackets

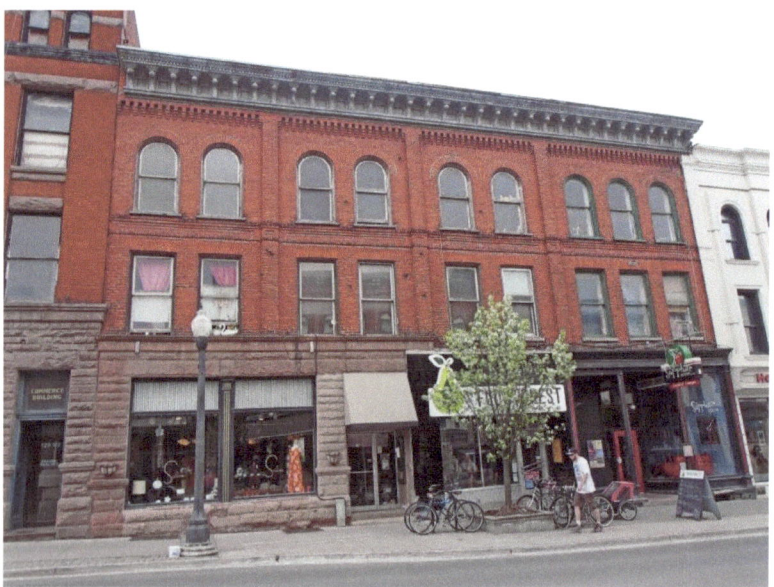

Hunter Street West - bevelled dentil moulding, pilasters

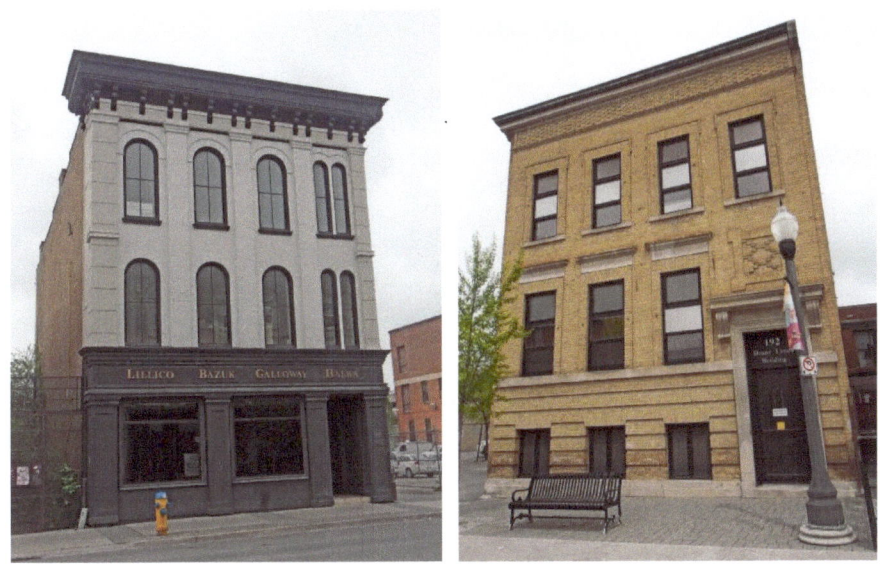

Hunter Street West
Cornice brackets, pilasters

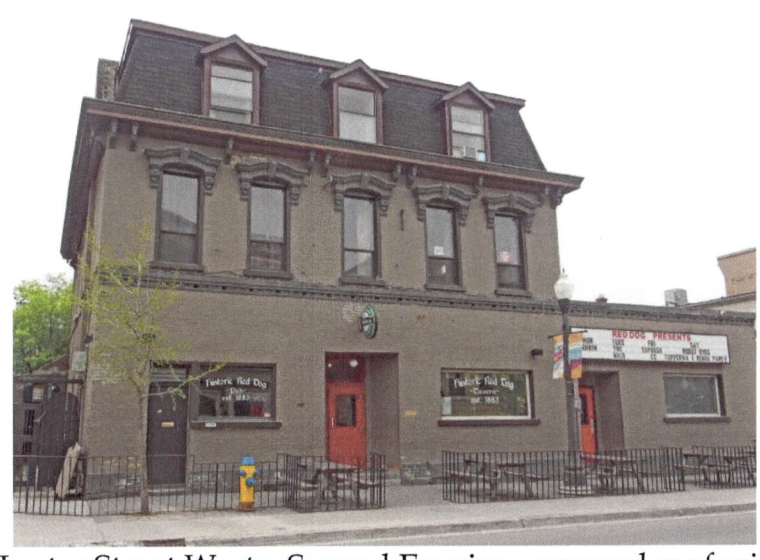

Hunter Street West – Second Empire, mansard roof with
dormers, cornice brackets, window hoods

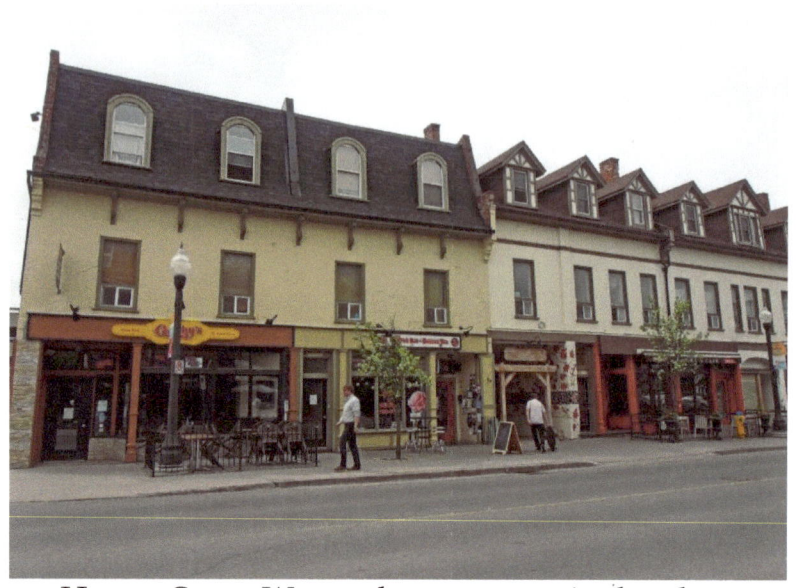

Hunter Street West – dormers, cornice brackets

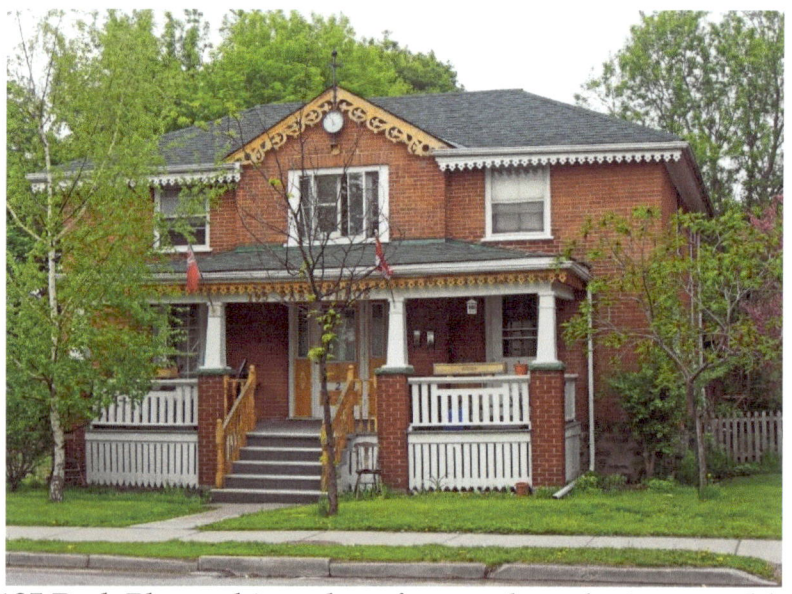

195 Park Place – hipped roof, verge board trim on gable

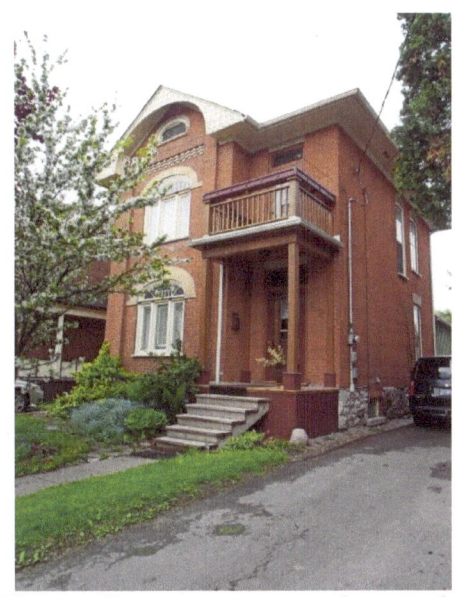

213 Park Place – Romanesque style window arches,
2nd floor balcony

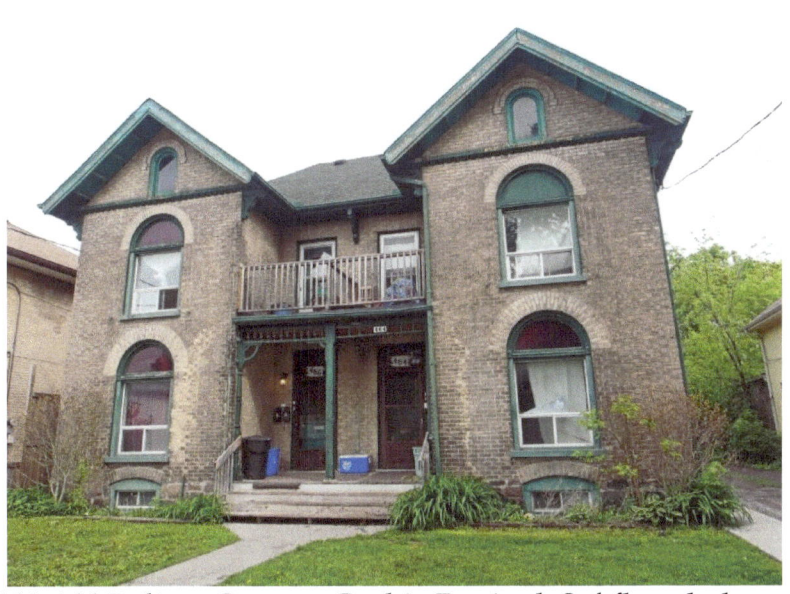

464-466 Bolivar Street – Gothic Revival, 2nd floor balcony

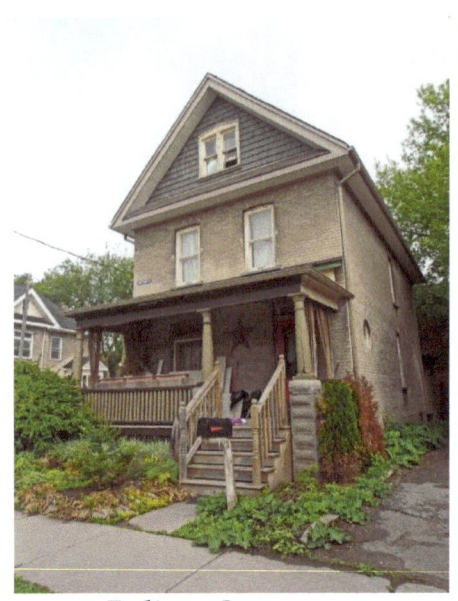

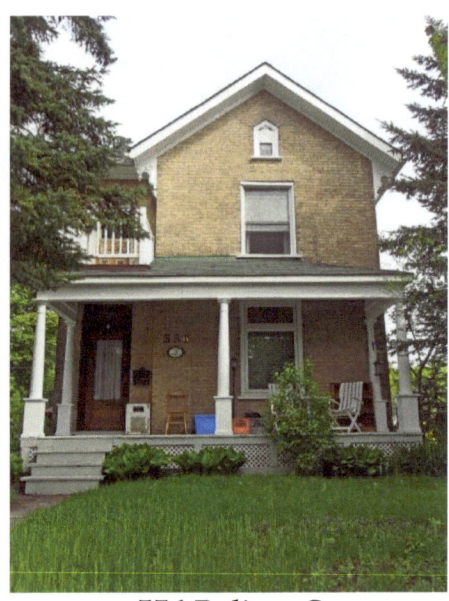

Bolivar Street
Edwardian

556 Bolivar Street
Gothic

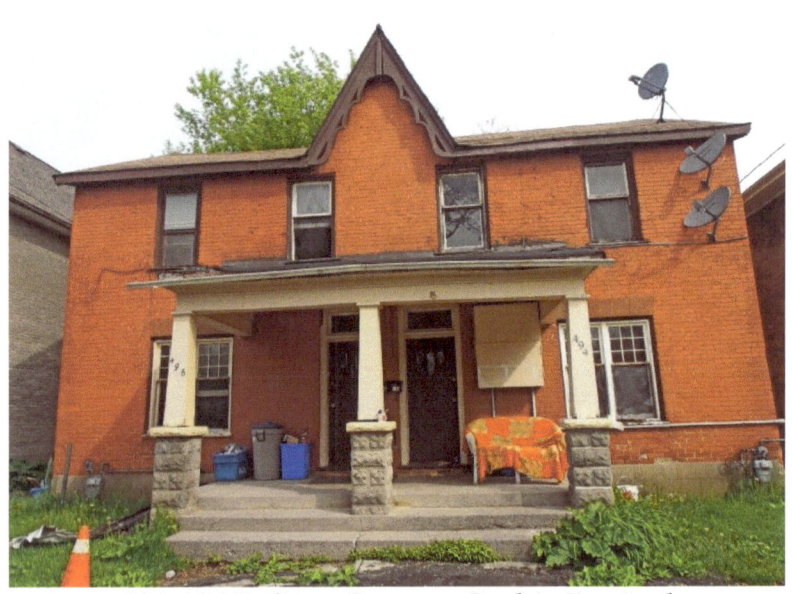

494-496 Bolivar Street – Gothic Revival

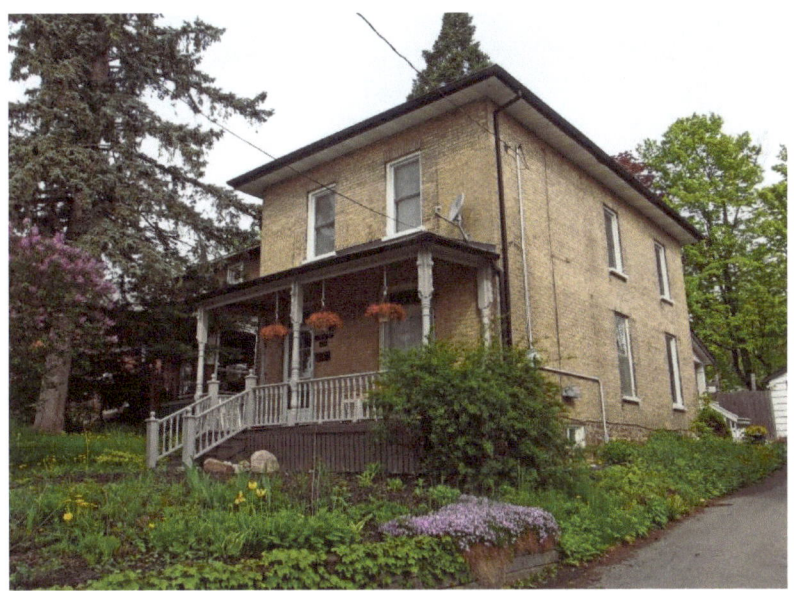

Bolivar Street - Italianate

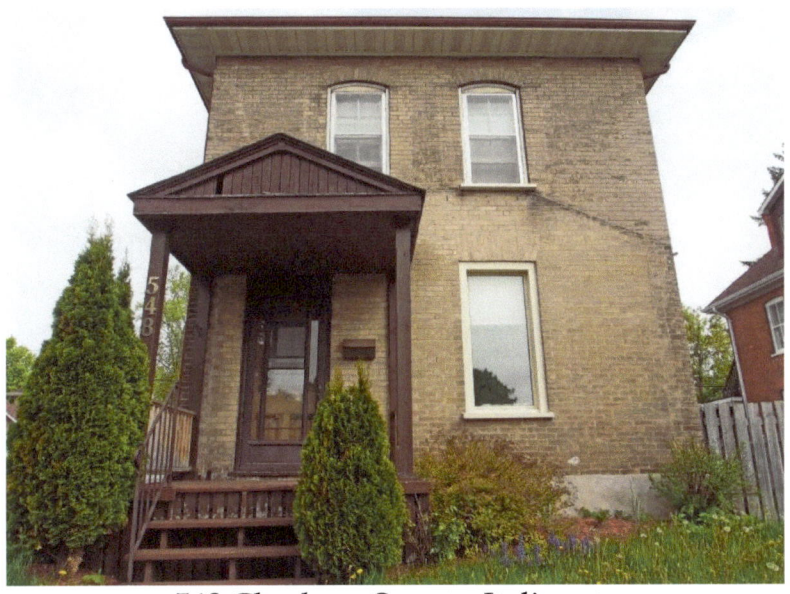

548 Charlotte Street - Italianate

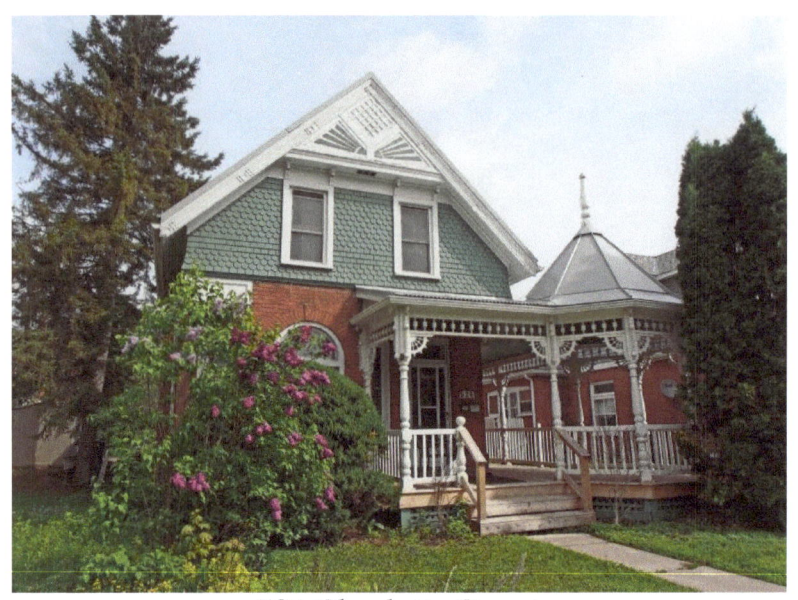

524 Charlotte Street

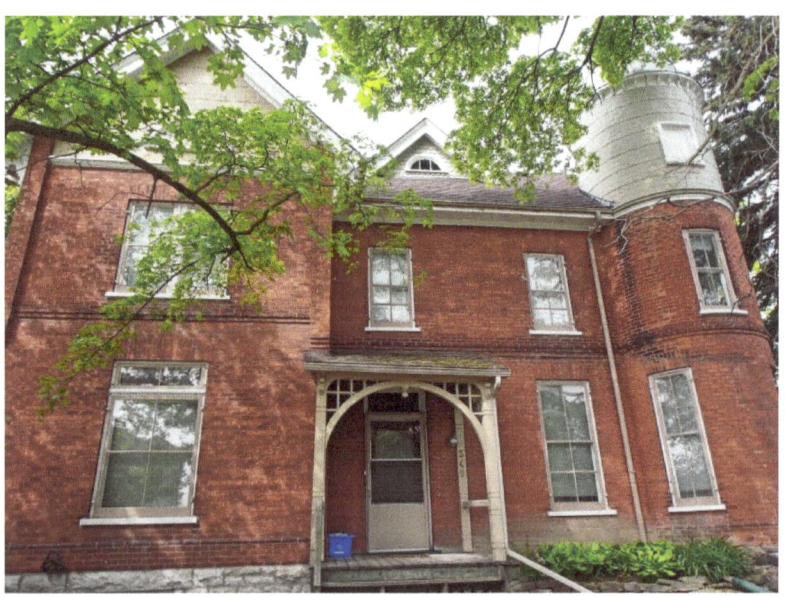

545 Charlotte Street – Queen Anne style with turret

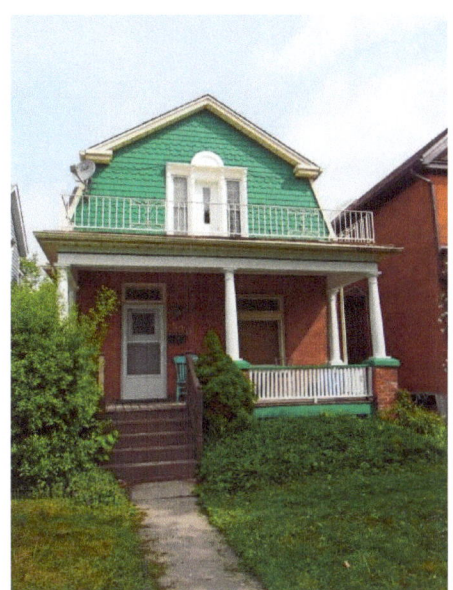

520 Charlotte Street

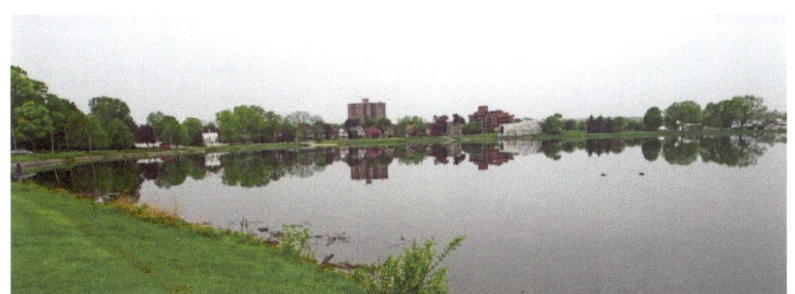

Little Lake reflections

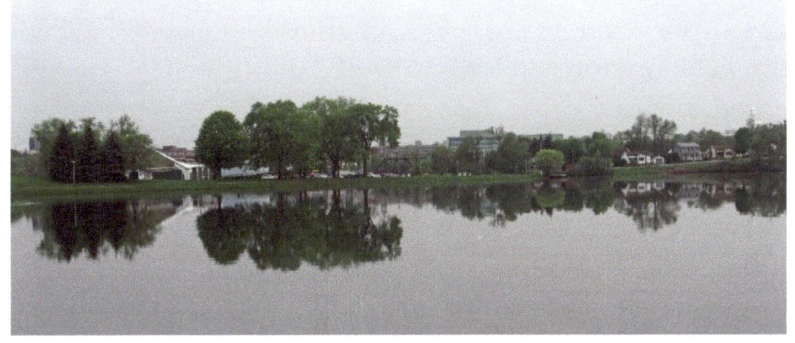

# Architectural Terms

| | |
|---|---|
| **Banding**: Different materials, colours or textures used in horizontal bands along a wall.<br><br>Example: 246-270 Rubidge Street | 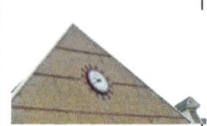 |
| **Brackets**: a decorative or weight-bearing structural element which forms a right angle with one side against a wall and the other under a projecting surface such as an eave or roof.<br>Example: George Street City Hall | 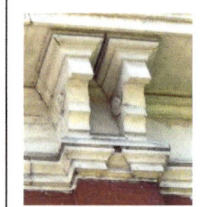 |
| **Buttress**: a masonry structure built against or projecting from a wall which serves to support or reinforce the wall. In Canadian architecture, they are sometimes used for decoration.<br>Example: 441 Rubidge Street | 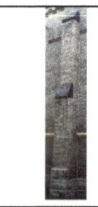 |
| **Capital:** The uppermost finish or decoration on a column. An Ionic column has a small base, a thin elegant shaft, and a capital composed of volutes which are carved whirls or twists that take the form of a scroll. A Doric column is characterized by a plain column with no base, a shaft with twenty flutings, and a simple capital with a simple entablature. A Corinthian column is characterized by a rounded capital decorated with acanthus leaves and a square abacus (the uppermost portion of a capital directly below the entablature) on tall slender columns.<br>Example: Ionic – George Street City Hall<br>Doric – 222 Rubidge Street<br>Corinthian – Simcoe Street | 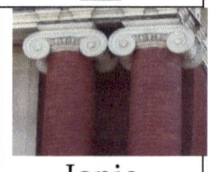<br>Ionic<br>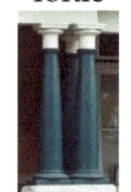<br>Doric<br>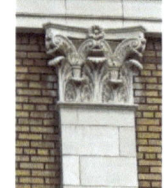<br>Corinthian |

| | |
|---|---|
| **Cornice**: originally the wooden overhang of the roof.  With the use of stone, brick, iron and steel, the cornice is any projecting shelf at the top of a ceiling or roof.  They can be very decorative.<br>Example: Water Street – see Page 47<br>Hunter Street West – see Page 53-54 | |
| **Dentil Moulding**: an even series of rectangles used as ornamental decoration in cornices.<br>Example: 441 Rubidge Street | |
| **Dichromatic brickwork**: the use of two colours of brick, tile or slate to decorate a façade.<br>Example: | |
| **Dormer**: (French for "sleep") a gable end window that pierces through the plane of a sloping roof surface to create usable space in the top floor or attic of a building by adding headroom.<br>Example:  Hunter Street West – see Page 57 | |
| **Fretwork:** interlaced decorative design resembling a bracket<br><br>Example: 224 Rubidge Street | |
| **Gable**: the triangular portion of a wall between the edges of a sloping roof.<br>Example:  Crescent Street – see Page 10 | |
| **Hipped Roof**: a roof where all sides slope downwards to the walls with no gables. | |

| | |
|---|---|
| **Keystones and Voussoirs**: a voussoir is a wedge-shaped element used in building an arch. A keystone is the central stone that locks all the stones into position, allowing the arch to bear weight. A keystone is often enlarged and embellished. Example: 565 George Street | |
| **Lancet Window**: a tall, narrow window with a pointed arch at its top.<br><br>Example: 441 Rubidge Street | |
| **Mansard Roof**: This style was popularized by Francois Mansart (1598-1666), an accomplished architect of the French Baroque period and especially fashionable during the Second French Empire (1852-1870). This roof is almost flat on the top section, with two slopes on each of its sides with the lower slope at a steeper angle than the upper and having dormer windows. Example: 332 Rubidge Street | |
| **Pediment**: a triangular section above the horizontal structure (entablature), typically supported by columns. The inside of the triangle is called the tympanum. Example: George Street | |
| **Pilaster**: a slightly projecting column built into or applied to the face of a wall for additional structural support. Example: | |

| | |
|---|---|
| **Quoin**: masonry blocks at the corner of a wall, often a decorative feature, usually larger or of a different colour than the rest of the wall. Example: 87 Lock Street – see Page 12 | 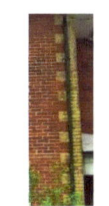 |
| **Rose Window:** a circular window with ornamental tracery radiating from the centre. Example: 441 Rubidge Street, St. Andrew's United Church | 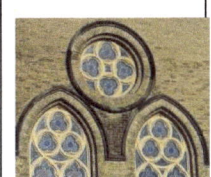 |
| **Turret:** a small tower that projects from the wall of a building. Example: 545 Charlotte Street | 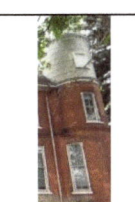 |
| **Verge board and Finial**: also called bargeboards – hang from the projecting end of a roof and are often elaborately carved and ornamented. **Finial:** ornament added to the top of a gable, pinnacle, canopy or spire – a Gothic element. Example: 270 Brock Street – see Pg. 8 | 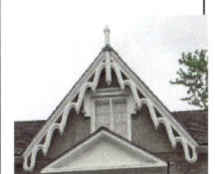 |
| **Window Hood:** A **hood** is the piece found above window openings, usually of an ornate design, and covers the top third of the opening. Hoods are commonly placed above arched or curved openings on both windows and doors. Example: Hunter Street West – see Page 54 | 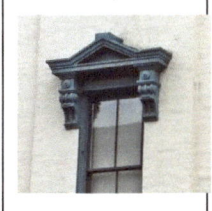 |

# Building Styles

| | |
|---|---|
| Classical Revival (1820 - 1860) – This style was an analytical, scientific, and dogmatic revival based on intensive studies of Greek and Roman buildings, concerned with the application of Greek plans and proportions to civic buildings. Schools, libraries, government offices, and most other civic buildings were built in the Classical Revival style. The white columned porches of the Classical Revival domestic buildings are identified with the mansions of wealthy land owners in Canada. Example: 413 Rubidge Street | 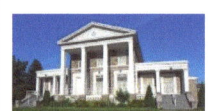 |
| Edwardian, 1900-1930 – This style bridges the ornate and elaborate styles of the Victorian era and the simplified styles of the 20th century. Balanced facades, simple roof lines, dormer windows, large front porches, and smooth brick surfaces are its characteristics. Example: 312 Rubidge Street, see Page 19 | 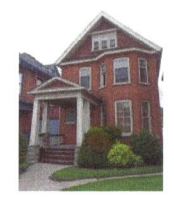 |
| Georgian, before 1860 – This style began with the British King Georges in the 18th century. These buildings have balanced facades around a central door, medium-pitched gable roofs, and small paned windows. Example: 599 Water Street, see Page 32 | 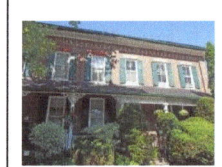 |
| Gothic Revival, 1830-1890 – These decorative buildings have sharply-pitched gables with highly detailed verge boards, pointed-arch window openings, and dichromatic brickwork. It is a common style in Ontario. Example:99 Brock Street – see Page 7 | 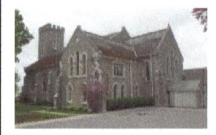 |

| | |
|---|---|
| Italianate, 1850-1900 – It has wide-bracketed eaves, belvederes, wrap-around verandahs.<br><br>Example: 232 Brock Street, see Page 9 | 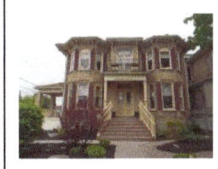 |
| Queen Anne, 1885-1900 – This style is distinguished by an irregular outline featuring a combination of an offset tower, broad gables, projecting two-storey bays, verandahs, multi-sloped roofs, and tall, decorative chimneys.  A mixture of brick and wood is common.  Windows often have one large single-paned bottom sash and small panes in the upper sash.  Example: 565 George Street, see Page 38 | 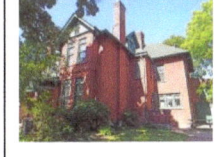 |
| Romanesque Revival, 1880-1910 – This style hearkens back to medieval architecture of the 11th and 12th centuries with a heavy appearance, blocky towers and rounded arches.  Example: 208 Romaine St., see Page 13 | 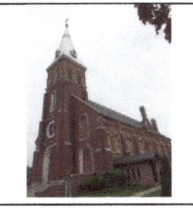 |
| Second Empire, 1860-1880 – The mansard roof is the most noteworthy feature of this style and is evidence of the French origins.  Projecting central towers and one or two-storey bays can also be present.<br>Example: 332-336 Rubidge Street | 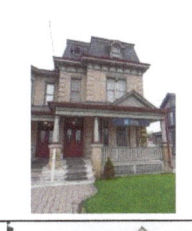 |
| Tudor Revival – exposed timbers with stucco infill, multi-paned windows.<br><br>Example: 208 Romaine Street – see Page 13 | |